FINDING
MEZCAL

You Don't Find Mezcal,
Mezcal Finds You

FINDING
MEZCAL

A Journey into the Liquid Soul of Mexico
WITH 40 COCKTAILS

**Ron Cooper, founder of Del Maguey
with Chantal Martineau**

PHOTOGRAPHY BY MICHAEL TOOLAN, KELLY PULEIO,
AND THE FRIENDS OF DEL MAGUEY

TEN SPEED PRESS
California | New York

CONTENTS

THE GETAWAY

The view out the windshield of my pickup is all sun-blasted blue sky and rocky clay-colored road. The tires kick up dirt, leaving clouds in the rearview. I've been driving for hours. Haven't seen another soul for miles. And here, up ahead, a little old man leading a stubby burro is coming my way. I slow down as we approach one another. He doesn't seem surprised to see me, even though vehicles are as rare as UFOs on these mountain roads. He waves. Everyone out here is courteous. As I come to a stop next to him and his hard-breathing animal, I lean way out the open window of my pickup and ask, "*Dónde está el mejor?*" Where is the best? He smiles. He knows what I mean. His response comes in a language that is not Spanish. His tribal tongue is guttural yet melodic, full of glottal stops, wheezy vowels, clicking consonants. He points a finger down the empty dirt road, the valley beyond. I get it, I think. I thank him, follow in the direction he pointed. In another couple hours, I confirm he wasn't shitting me. I find what I've been looking for: mezcal.

This is Oaxaca, my heart home. I first traveled here on a dare in 1970. I'd just done a group show in Los Angeles curated by the art dealer Riko Mizuno, a tough Japanese woman and the meanest poker player in town. After the opening, she and I, along with the artist Jim Ganzer and the Malibu surfboard shaper Robbie Dick, sat down with a bottle of the only good tequila available in the United States at the time. After a few too many shots, someone at the table—and none of us remembers who—said, "I wonder if the Pan-American Highway really exists?" The next morning, instead of nursing a hangover or surrendering to postblackout amnesia, I let the seed of that question plant itself inside me. It germinated. Within a fortnight, I was on a young man's adventure with Jim and Robbie, tearing down the fabled Pan-American Highway in a VW van. We took it all the way to Panama, windows rolled down, hot air pouring in like lion's breath. We drove through Mexico, Guatemala, Honduras, El Salvador, Nicaragua, and Costa Rica, bouncing along on rocks and dirt. The trip took four months. By the time we got to Panama and saw blacktop again, it was like, *Shit! We made it!* Along the way, we stopped in small towns and along beaches to hang out and surf. One of those towns was Oaxaca.

Back then, Oaxaca had few tourists. Nowadays, foreigners show up to fill their suitcases with folk art and their bellies with mole. But in the early 1970s, the locals were surprised to see three gringos passing through. I had a thick handlebar mustache as black as my long hair and wide-open eyes that wanted to drink in every little thing. Man, it was a wild scene. Oaxaqueños still wore white pegged cotton pants and loose pullover shirts with sombreros and *huaraches*. The women were decked out in colorful woven prints—boxy tunics called *huipiles* or long skirts and almost always a *rebozo*, the ubiquitous scarf worn in a million different ways, as both fashion statement and makeshift carrier of babies and other bundles. Only a few people had store-bought shoes. My two friends and I soaked it all in. The handmade pottery, the hand-woven textiles. We heard about a village—Teotitlán del Valle—where spectacular weavings were made about an hour's drive from the city. We went to check it out. There we met a family of weavers and befriended their teenage son, Arnulfo Mendoza. Arnulfo would grow up to be the greatest weaver in Mexico.

Twenty years later, in 1990, after I'd made some fuck-you money from two big Los Angeles art commissions—enough to go anywhere I wanted for three months—I had my heart set on seeing Japan. Ever since I was ten years old, I'd wanted to go there. As a kid, I was into sumo wrestlers and Zen philosophy. Finally, I was going to fly over the Pacific and land in Tokyo and it was going to be incredible. But just as my Japanese odyssey was unfolding in my mind's eye, it was interrupted. From somewhere deep within, a voice I couldn't ignore was saying, *No, no, no. You're not going to Japan. You're going back to Mexico. You're going to collaborate with indigenous craftspeople. You're going to make art.* And that's how I ended up losing myself down the backroads of Oaxaca.

Once I'd made the decision to go, Arnulfo Mendoza was the first person I called. I'd been back to Oaxaca to visit a couple times since we'd first met, and he'd come up to Los Angeles for an exhibition of traditional Zapotec weavings organized by mutual friends in the mid-1970s. Now he was a serious artist. Arnulfo had spent some time in Japan, where he'd learned to weave silk kimonos, and had returned to Oaxaca to open the first gallery and weaving workshop in the city center. I asked if he knew where I could get a house and he said, "I'll give you a house." I packed all my tools and drawings into a four-wheel-drive Ford pickup and hit the road. From Taos, New Mexico, where I live, it's about a thirty-hour drive nowadays. Back then, the roads were a lot worse and it took a good deal longer. Arnulfo put me up in a two-story house on Calle Macedonio Alcalá in Oaxaca City, just off Avenida Benito Juárez. If you take that road all the way out of town, it turns into the Pan-American Highway. Arnulfo's two brothers stayed on the first floor from time to time, but I had the whole top floor to myself. I set up my tools and materials and got to work. For three full months, I made art. Weavings, paintings on tin, etchings, stone sculpture, wood sculpture. It was the most joyous time of my life. I experienced the freest, most spontaneous period of creativity imaginable. I made art out of everything, and everything I touched was art.

Vessels were already a recurring theme in my work. I'd been making lamps and bronze vases that dealt with the concept of negative space. I envisioned a sculptural edition of fifty handblown blue glass bottles shaped in the image of Ometochtli, the ancient supreme god of intoxication and ecstasy. The bottles would be filled with the local elixir, a spirit distilled from the native agave plant. Mezcal was a part of every fiesta Arnulfo took me to—births, deaths, weddings, religious holidays. Mezcal was how people celebrated, communed, honored their loved ones and the dead. I decided I'd fill my blue glass bottles with the best mezcal I could find.

I continued to work on my weavings and etchings and paintings, but every third day, I'd take a dirt road out of town and just drive. When someone crossed my path, like the old man with his burro, I'd stop and ask, "Where's the best?" *Dónde está el mejor?* I never asked, "Where's the best mezcal?" I didn't have to. I'd just smile and say, "Where's the best?" and the stranger would smile back, completely understanding me. Much gesticulating would follow, a finger pointing me down a signless road. I spoke a little Spanish, but it was of no use to me here. These were Zapotec or Mixe or Mixteca Indians, speaking in ancient dialects that have nothing to do with Spanish. I couldn't understand their language, but I followed where their fingers pointed. I went over mountains, across rivers, descended into valleys, driving four, eight, twelve hours. Sometimes I would come to a fork in the dirt road and have to guess which path to take. I'd sniff the air, close my eyes, let my instincts guide me. Finally, I would see, out in the distance, a big stone grinding wheel used to press agave. And I knew I was in the right place.

"How do you make this stuff?" I asked the men hard at work in the *palenques*, the rustic open-air distilleries I came upon. These structures—with no electricity and, oftentimes, no walls—housed the primitive equipment used to make mezcal. The men showed me fields filled with agave, the perennial succulents they called *maguey* (pronounced *MA-gay*) from which mezcal is made. These were the colossal cactus-like plants I'd seen sprouting from the hills. Some of the men went deep into the forest or combed the steep, brambly hillsides to harvest wild maguey. Others farmed it in rough-hewn orchards or bought it from agave farmers they knew and trusted. They taught me how to distinguish one variety from another, how to tell when a plant is ripe. It can take ten, fifteen, twenty, thirty years, depending on the variety. They showed me how they loaded the maguey hearts—*piñas* because they look like pineapples—into the *horno*, the oven (a conical stone-lined pit dug into the ground). The men covered the maguey hearts with spent maguey fibers and earth, and let them roast for four or five days. When the roast was done, they let the maguey rest in the shade for a week. They crushed the caramelized maguey in a primitive mill, a large round stone pit affixed with a one-ton wheel carved out of stone in the center. The stone was pulled by a horse or mule, around and around, grinding the roasted maguey. (In tequila, this wheel is known as a *tahona*, but that word means nothing here in Oaxaca.) In some palenques, the maguey was mashed in a hollowed-out tree trunk by a man with thick hands and a hefty ironwood bat or mallet. The pulpy mash and fibers were collected and fed into open wooden tanks.

"How do you ferment?" I asked. "What makes this thing change into alcohol? Don't you put anything in it?"

"*No! No!*" They exclaimed. "*No levaduras! Puro! Primero dios!*" Pure, they said. No added yeast. Fermented by the power of the first deity—Mother Nature. Rather than adding synthetically produced beer or Champagne or bread yeast, as distillers of other spirits do, they fermented the maguey with wild strains occurring naturally in the environment. Over days or weeks, depending on the weather, the mixture fermented. The tanks bubbled and steamed. I understood, as the crude saying goes, that "yeasts eat sugar, piss alcohol, and fart carbon dioxide." When the wild yeasts completed their job, the musts and fibers were scooped into small copper stills. In some villages, the stills were made of clay.

The mezcal I tasted in these distant villages was different from what I had at Arnulfo's family's fiestas. Pure and clean, it tasted of desert air and wild grasses, of earth and sky. Some were sweet and fruity, some spicy, some funky, some rich, some delicate. They had flavors I'd never encountered before, but even more extraordinary was the effect this mezcal had on me. It helped crack open my mind and spirit, allowing me to tap into the soft, pulsing source of my creativity like nothing ever had or would again. I understood it as art, plain and simple. A work of art is successful to me if it causes an "aha" moment, if it transforms the viewer. A nude, a still life, a construction of garbage, a bunch of words—it doesn't matter what it is, so long as it's transformative. The mezcal I encountered had the power to transform.

As I spent more time in palenques and among *palenqueros*, I began to understand the ritual uses of mezcal. It was taken in celebration; to mark births, deaths, and marriages; and as part of tribal ceremonies. Drops of it were given to young children to fortify them. I watched the women past childbearing age leaving the market in the morning, carrying baskets of foodstuffs on their heads and flowers for their altars, stop at a rough-plank counter in a *tienda*—a small, funky shop—across the street on their way home. An ounce of mezcal cured with herbs dulled the pain

FRESH-CUT *MAGUEY* NEXT TO THE FIRE
OF THE SMOLDERING *HORNO*.

of being on their knees grinding corn all day or the onset of arthritis. Mezcal was sacred. It was curative. They called it *medicina*.

When it came time to taste the clear spirit that dripped out from a narrow tube protruding from the belly of the still, the men always performed the same ritual. Collecting it in a hollowed-out gourd called a *jícara*, they used a dried bamboo-like reed as a straw to suck up the liquid, though not enough to let it touch their lips. Instead, placing a thumb over the opening of the reed, known as a *venencia*, the mezcal would remain trapped inside until the thumb was removed and the spirit released. As it streamed back into the jícara, tight round bubbles formed on the surface of the liquid. "*Perlas*," the men explained. Pearls. These were the mark of a good mezcal. To the trained eye, the perlas indicated the precise proof of the spirit. Their size, clarity, and how quickly they dissipated could be read like a hydrometer. The proof rarely clocked in below 45 percent alcohol by volume (ABV). No water was added. "*Mezcal con agua no es mezcal*," I was told.

Over three months, I gathered twenty-eight samples of mezcal from different palenqueros around the state of Oaxaca. I filled whatever empty bottle I could find— used Pedro Domecq brandy bottles, Bacardi rum bottles, old Coke bottles, the original Raymond Loewy design sealed with a corncob stopper. I'd go back to Teotitlán del Valle to share what I found with Arnulfo. He was dumbfounded. We drank mezcal together regularly, at the end of the day as we looked over how the weavings were progressing. But he had never tasted anything like the mountain mezcal I brought him. The *pueblos* (villages) they came from—San Pedro Ixtlahuaca, Sola de Vega, San Andrés Zabache—were foreign to him. But the liquid was somehow not. Sipping it felt like coming home, for us both. "Where did you get this?" Arnulfo would ask me in disbelief. "You're the Zapotec!" I joked with him. But he'd never heard of the remote pueblos I traveled to for mezcal.

As the end of my three months in Oaxaca neared, there was a wedding. I'd befriended a second family of Zapotec weavers in Teotitlán del Valle, the Martínezes. The second-youngest of four brothers, Sergio, was to be wed. Because I had the only vehicle in town, I was enlisted to ferry the bride's family around, transport beer and mezcal, pick up oversize corn tortillas called *tlayudas* from the market in nearby Tlacolula de Matamoros, and run other errands. The wedding lasted eight days. There was drinking, dancing, feasting, praying, gift giving, more drinking, more dancing. By the end of the week, the family had adopted me into their clan. At the end of the eight-day celebration, Cosme, the patriarch, asked me to do him a great favor. He wanted me to take his eldest son, Pancho, across the US border with me. Against my better judgment, I agreed. As a show of gratitude, he gave me a five-gallon jug of the special mezcal he'd served at the wedding. I never learned who made it, but clearly it had been made with great care and most likely had been aged in black clay jugs, called *cántaros*. It came cradled in a handwoven wicker basket to protect against breakage.

Before I left Oaxaca to return to Taos, I decided to throw a farewell party. I invited all the people I'd met and collaborated with—artisans, painters, sculptors, potters, carpenters, and all my weaver friends. I rented a marimba, and, as caterers, I hired the local women whose street tacos and *memelitas* (open-faced corn tortillas topped with lard, beans, and cheese) I loved. We even had cocktails: coconuts sliced open, their sweet juice spiked with mezcal. My guests, all Zapotec Indians, had never been to a party like this before. Put together by a gringo, the fiesta's familiar components merged to feel exotic.

The festivities didn't start winding down until midmorning the next day. I spent that entire day packing my pickup. By dusk, it was loaded ten feet high, filled with all the art I'd made and the crafts I'd collected. It was then, with the last stragglers refusing to let the party die, that Pancho showed up. When he walked in, everyone went quiet. And that's how I learned that the Martínezes and the Mendozas were mortal enemies—like the Hatfields and the McCoys. Arnulfo and his family were my oldest friends in Oaxaca; I'd been living in their house for the three months. When they found out I was taking Pancho to the United States, they were stunned and a little affronted. But I couldn't renege on my vow.

I left Teotitlán del Valle that night with Pancho in the passenger's seat. The bed of my

ABOVE: A JUG OF MEZCAL CAPPED WITH A CORN COB.
BELOW: PANCHO.

pickup was overflowing, the precious jug of wedding mezcal tucked in safely on one side. We drove in the dark, stopping at a nameless roadside stand to fortify ourselves with eggs, beans, and tortillas cooked over a wood fire. And here was Pancho, telling me his life story. He'd been a boxer and a weaver. Now he had two young daughters. It wouldn't be his first time crossing the border; he'd picked strawberries in California several seasons back. But it would be his final adventure. He hoped to return to his village before his daughters were old enough to miss him. My Spanish was horrendous and he spoke Zapotec-village Spanish, learned as a second language to communicate with the outside world. Yet we managed to understand each other. In a short time, we became friends.

In 1990, Mexico was different. What is now a four-lane highway was a narrow two-way road. Besides rickety buses, mine was the only vehicle for miles. The people we passed wore traditional garb. They led oxcarts burdened with firewood or the freshly harvested crops they were carrying home from their fields. Pancho and I spent our first night in a mountain town hotel, a stately, if rundown, manor with columns and an interior courtyard. The rooms were furnished with hard beds and even harder pillows. We returned to the truck the next morning to find a police officer waiting for us. No one had told me I would need a special permit to haul anything above the level of my pickup's box. The cop said he'd have to impound my truck if I couldn't produce the proper paperwork. Of course, that's not what he really wanted. We ended up giving him a couple hundred pesos, maybe twenty bucks, and he let us go. A couple miles down the road, we were stopped a second time. Hours later, it happened again. And again. And again. I don't know how many times we were pulled over that day, but each time was the same. The cops all wanted their *mordida*, their little bite.

By nightfall, we made it to Querétaro, a small state north of Mexico City. We were mulling our next move when a Volkswagen Vocho (the local nickname for the Beetle) drove up next to us and two undercover cops pulled out guns—fucking Colt magnums, like Clint Eastwood carried. Exasperation got the better of me. "That's it! Fuck you!" I started yelling. "I'm broke! You guys have stolen all my fucking money! You're all motherfucking assholes!" The cops were amused. They lowered their weapons and asked us to follow them to a nearby hotel with a fenced-in parking area. They told the front desk to put us up for the night, free of charge.

The next morning, as we got back on the road, I started to wonder how the hell I was going to get Pancho across the border. More importantly, where to cross? There was nothing but desert ahead. I didn't want to go to Juárez or Nuevo Laredo, both known drug crossings. Then on the map I spotted a small town called Ojinaga. I remembered it from the movie *The Getaway* and thought, *Yeah, that's the place!* The plot went like this: after a bloody bank robbery, Ali MacGraw and Steve McQueen highjack a 1950s Chevy pickup. They force the driver, a cowpoke played by Slim Pickens, to drive them to Mexico. Along the way, the three end up forging a friendship and the couple pays the cowboy thirty thousand bucks for his old truck. He goes home happily on foot and the heroes cross the border at Ojinaga, disappearing into Mexico with their bagfuls of money. (The film held special significance for me. Back in the day, Jim Ganzer and I had each dated one of director Sam Peckinpah's two daughters. Peckinpah was a cool cat with a chiseled face and an impenetrable air. His daughters were both blonde, bronzed California beauties. One gray afternoon, Jim and I were invited to San Marcos, Texas, where Peckinpah was filming, for gin-and-tonics in honor of his birthday. We were on our way back from the peyote fields of Star County, where we'd spent several days, my Citroën Pallas still littered with buttons. After a few too many drinks, Peckinpah demanded that we stay for dinner. Slim Pickens and Rip Torn would be joining us. We would have loved to stay, we said, but had to politely decline on account of already having plans to take his daughters to dinner. He flew into a rage, whipped out a pistol, cocked it, and pointed it directly at my chest. "Don't let the door hit you in the ass on the way out," he said. We got the fuck out of there.)

I'd only set eyes on the towns in Texas directly across the border—Valentine, Marfa, Presidio—but I was convinced: Ojinaga was the shit. I hatched a plan to do as MacGraw and McQueen did in the movie, only the reverse, escaping with Pancho into the United States. The turnoff for Ojinaga takes you through flat, unmerciful desert. After hours on the road, we came to a mining town. Famished, we headed to the only place in town to eat, a cafeteria with pine paneling and no sign. It existed pretty much solely to feed the miners who were all back at work. We ate quickly. Waiting for us outside were more than a dozen vigilantes, standing guard around my pickup. They began questioning us, suspecting us of drug trafficking. Pancho and I had developed this game whenever we were in trouble: I spoke fake Zapotec and he replied in real Zapotec so neither of us appeared to speak Spanish. It threw people off and kept sketchy interactions brief.

We talked our way out of the standoff and got the hell out of town. The road to Ojinaga stretched out before us, hot and long. We arrived, thirsty and bone-tired, just in time to witness a violent sandstorm kick up. It was a sweet little town that could have been plucked from any old Western. On the main plaza, though, we realized that every single person around us was armed with an Uzi. Now Pancho and I understood why the vigilantes a hundred-fifty miles back were so alarmed at us passing through. We had chosen what turned out to be one of the biggest drug crossings in Mexico for our little crime.

Warily, we walked into the local billiard parlor. The swinging saloon doors screeched, announcing our presence, and everyone inside looked up. The place was silent save for the crack-crack-cracking of billiard balls. All eyes were on us. We ordered a couple cold beers and downed them hastily. I mentioned to one of the friendlier looking barflies that we were looking to get Pancho across the border. A cab driver within earshot offered to introduce us to a friend of his, a coyote (smuggler of illegal aliens). We left my pickup behind and drove out into the countryside with this stranger. The coyote turned out to be a young guy, harmless enough, at least it seemed. After a little banal chit-chat, it was time to make a deal. I was to wait at a certain motel in Presidio, Texas, directly across the border. Pancho would be delivered at eleven o'clock that night. I pulled out a hundred-dollar bill I'd kept hidden from all the corrupt cops we'd encountered since Oaxaca and, staring the coyote down, I tore it in half.

"I'll give you the other half when I see Pancho again," I told him.

Pancho and I said good-bye in the sandstorm, the wind and dust whipping around us like a cloak. By this time, we'd been together a full three days. The pain of parting caught us off-guard. We'd grown attached to one another, and I could see that he was terrified. I was, too. "I'll see you on the other side," I assured him as we embraced, both of us hoping it was true.

From Ojinaga, it's a short drive to the border. The US customs agent took one look at my pickup piled high with arts and crafts and went, "What's all this shit?" and "Who the hell are you?" I replied, "I'm Ron Cooper. I'm an artist from Taos. I've been in Oaxaca making art for three months." Blank stare. "Well, what's that there in the bottle?" the agent asked, pointing to my five-gallon jug of wedding mezcal. I started rhapsodizing to the man about this amazing elixir I'd discovered and the pure-hearted farmers who made it. I tried to tell him about the way it tastes of the desert and splits the mind wide open like overripe fruit. His face showed only scorn. "Boy, you can't bring that shit in here," he drawled. "W-w-w-wait!" I stuttered. "I'll pay any duty you want!" He was unmoved. "As a US citizen, you can bring *one* liter of alcohol across the border," he told me. "And that's it. So, you can go back to Mexico and drink that shit or you can pour it out right here down this here hole." And with that, he pointed his finger at a drain used for discarding contraband alcohol. I had no choice.

Through tears, I heard the *glug-glug-glug* of the cherished wedding mezcal swirling down the drain. I poured it out slowly, mourning each ounce as it disappeared to god-knows-where. As I was pouring, I heard the agent walk away behind me. I didn't turn around to confirm he was out of sight, but, holding my breath, I took a chance and stopped pouring. I was still hunched over the drain, clutching the jug, frozen. There were about two gallons of mezcal left inside. I tried to get my eyes to see beyond the limits of my peripheral vision, to swerve around the back of my head, but I couldn't tell where the agent had gone. The hairs on the back of my neck stood on end and my ears perked up as, cautiously, I rose from my crouched position. Silently, I placed the bottle back in its wicker basket and crept back to the truck. I gently squeezed the door's handle; it let out a high-pitched wheeze as it opened. I was waiting to get shot in the back or at least seriously reprimanded. But no one seemed to notice me slide into the driver's seat. I tried to catch sight of the customs agent in the rearview mirror, but he was nowhere to be seen. I closed the door as quietly as possible—*click*—and fired up the engine. No one was after me. I stepped heavily on the gas pedal and in seconds I was out of Mexico, leaving behind nothing but a cloud of dust.

That was the moment I decided that no one would ever again tell me I couldn't bring mezcal into the United States. I would do whatever it took to ensure that never again would I be forced to pour good mezcal down the drain.

It was the dead of summer, about seven o'clock at night, and still 110°F out. By the time I checked into the motel in Presidio, I was hungry, sweaty, drained. In my room, the air-conditioning was on full blast. Hunger won out over exhaustion, so I went in search of food. Locating the motel restaurant, I pulled open the heavy air-locked door. And before me, to my stomach-sinking shock, were some fifty Border Patrol agents, just sitting there, shooting the shit. I didn't scream, but I wanted to. Instead, wordlessly, I backed out of the restaurant, hurried back to the room, left the key on the bed, and got back into my truck. As I sped away, I noticed that not only was it the wrong motel, but also across the street were a succession of trailers: mobile jails for people coming across the border illegally.

A little further down the road was another motel, a funky low ranch house with a pool. An entire family of Mexicans, all fat—*gordos*—were floating in it. As my truck crunched onto the gravel driveway, a hefty young woman got out and, still dripping, checked me in. The wooden porch steps to my room squeaked as I climbed them, and the screen door creaked as it swung open. Inside was an old iron bed with a lumpy spring mattress and a fan overhead. *Wooo-renk, wooo-renk* went the fan. *Fuck it*, I thought to myself, and fell into bed. Forget eating or even cracking open the mezcal I'd managed to smuggle into the country. Instead, I would just wait for Pancho in front of the black-and-white TV. Letterman was on. Before long, I surrendered to a blackout sleep. I was awakened hours later by the vicious barking of dogs. The whir of the fan, the loud baying of dogs, and the ghostly crackle of snow on the idle television set had an orchestral effect. I nodded off again and when I awoke, it was past eleven. Pancho still hadn't shown up.

Sleep engulfed me once more and terrifying scenarios began plaguing my dreams. When I woke up for good, it was six o'clock in the morning and the sun was already blazing. The air was thick, the fan providing little relief from the heat. I realized that what had roused me was the distant sound of Ritchie Valens blaring from a car stereo. *BAM-ba bamba! BAM-ba bamba!* Out front, a lowrider pulled up and coughed out a muddy, shivering Pancho. I ushered him inside before handing the coyote the other half of the hundred-dollar bill. He and his friends all laughed as they tore off down the road. Pancho told me how they had tried to cross, but Border Patrol agents had shown up and they were forced to turn back. He and the coyote had hidden inside an old car in a backyard all night, freezing their asses off. But now he'd made it. He was okay.

We got on the road soon after. I pulled my seat forward so Pancho could lie on the floor behind it. I covered him with a map, a sombrero, and a towel, and headed toward Marfa. Not two dozen miles out, to my horror, I spotted a border checkpoint in the distance. Outside a tiny stilt house, two agents sat having their morning coffee in the sunshine. "Don't move, Pancho," I growled through clenched teeth. Just as I was about to start slowing down to be questioned, a white Chevy Suburban came flying past me, weaving in and out of lanes. It was some drunk the agents must have known because they started shaking their heads and slapping their knees, doubled over in laughter. They waved at the lush as he swerved past and were so busy giggling they barely noticed me drive by. Pancho and I breathed a sigh of relief as we rolled on toward Marfa, then up into the hills. Once we were well out of town on a deserted stretch of road, I stopped the truck. I helped poor Pancho get up from his cramped, contorted position. We stepped outside with the cup from a thermos and stretched. I poured us some mezcal out of my five-gallon jug that still had two gallons left in it and we toasted our triumph.

The spirit tasted sweet, like a memory, out there by the side of the road. Weary and frayed as we were, it restored us. As we sipped in silence, its aromas transported us to the place where our journey began, all desert-mountain and salty air. In New Mexico, where we were headed, Pancho would become my right-hand man. My *pistolero*. The two of us would return to this mezcal, filling our *copitas* (glasses) with a sense of reverence and ceremony, whenever he needed a taste of home.

We continued our journey to Las Cruces, then Albuquerque, through Chimayó, and finally up to Taos. I put Pancho up in an Airstream trailer I had behind my studio. He stayed with me, assisting me in my work. His father was pleased. After about three months, Pancho decided to take a bus up to Denver and got a job as a busboy at a bar that was the unofficial team hangout of the Denver Broncos. He was so proud. Three years later, his father called me. "Hey, I want my son back!" he barked. It was time to send Pancho home.

ALTAR AT THE STILL, SAN LUIS DEL RÍO.

CHAPTER 1

LIGHT, SPACE, AND LIQUID

In 1950, after the Mexican section of the Pan-American Highway was completed, the Mexican government staged the Carrera Panamericana: the Pan-American Road Race. The idea was to show off the new road and prove how modern the country was becoming. For the first time ever, it was possible to drive from one end of Mexico to the other on pavement. Before that, it was all narrow-gauge railroads, dirt roads, a few paved roads, but very hard going for anyone who dared to travel. As it turned out, the road race was deadly. Conditions were rough and crashes abounded. The race was discontinued after a few years and too many fatalities, only to be revived in the 1980s. It was no less treacherous the second time around.

In another lifetime, I might have raced the Panamericana instead of exploring it at my leisure. Before becoming an artist, I built and raced cars. I didn't grow up thinking I'd be an artist. For the better part of my teens, I had my heart set on becoming the world's greatest custom car builder. I came into the world on a midsummer's day in 1943 in the Kew Gardens neighborhood of Queens in New York City. My father served in the Second World War as a medic's assistant, carrying dead and dying bodies from the battlefield to the medical tents. He came back from the war a changed man. One day in the late 1940s, a blizzard hit New York. My father walked in from the storm covered in snow, his frosted eyelashes almost frozen shut. My mother put him to bed with my three-year-old brother and a glass of Scotch. She came in a little while later to check on my dad and found him fast asleep. My baby brother had swallowed the whiskey. When my father woke up, he announced his decision as if he'd just dreamed it: "We're moving to California."

My father, mother, brother, and I drove across the country to the West Coast in the family car, a 1949 two-door Ford sedan. I was seven years old. My dad went into business with a friend, opening a carpet store in Ventura. My mother, who comes from a family of creatives and intellectuals, decided the only place she cared to live was Ojai. The small, rustic town lay some eighty miles northwest of Los Angeles. It was a bohemian paradise. The ceramicist Beatrice Wood and the spiritual writer Jiddu Krishnamurti made their lives there. It had one of the country's first vegetarian restaurants, where they made stone-ground, whole-wheat bread. Ojai offered an alternative way of being. Once we settled in, I started looking at life in a new way. My parents did, too. They hung a long horizontal print—black ink on handmade oatmeal-colored paper—of an ancient Japanese stone carving on the living room wall.

Ojai existed outside many norms. It's one of the only valleys in California that runs east-west rather than north-south, and its sunsets are known to linger, bright pink. You look up at the sky and see condors—fucking condors!—flying overhead.

I was impressed by its burgeoning community of people who wanted to live a different life than the one they'd lived before. They, like us, came seeking refuge. They wished to live by their own rules and wits. By and large, they were artists, writers, philosophers, idealists. They started their own schools that did not follow the curriculum fed to so many kids around the country. They grew their own fruits and vegetables, made their own clothes. In 1950, the town's population was 2,500 and growth was controlled by the town council. The newcomers were fiercely protective of their Shangri-La, even though it wasn't theirs to begin with. Ojai was already inhabited by people who lived close to the earth and at a remove from the rest of the world. The Chumash Indians gave the Ojai Valley its name, which comes from their word for "moon." Their way of life provided inspiration and romance for the new bohemian class. The town was also home to a mestizo Mexican community. But the three groups existed independently from one another.

My first girlfriend—or what passes for a girlfriend at eleven years old—was the daughter of a Chumash Indian chief, the last true medicine man in town. Even then, I was drawn to cool people. I had no interest in the boring kids who all dressed and talked alike. My mother put me in Happy Valley School, a private school based on the Socratic method of teaching. No lectures. Instead, the teachers asked us questions, encouraging us to find the answers that dwelled within. Aldous Huxley, Alan Watts, and Jiddu Krishnamurti sat on the board of directors. My parents wanted me to be a nerd, but I was a bad student. I spent my time hiding out in the library reading *National Geographic* and daydreaming. I did miserably in Spanish. But when my parents drove us down to Tijuana, taking the narrow two-lane road that snaked through the avocado and orange orchards of Santa Ana, I was the only one with any Spanish words. I was the translator. A year later, we drove to Mazatlán by way of Arizona. There was only one hotel in town and the Coke machine spat out bottles for just five cents. I was the translator once again. It was around this time that I started falling in love with Mexican culture.

Despite living in Ojai, an environment where creativity and free thinking thrived, I gravitated toward the speed-thirsty world of car racing. In high school, I had two totally bitchin' cars, a black Ford pickup that I used to drag race and this beautiful Buick Century two-door coupe, black with a white roof, for cruising around. I was also in the local chapter of 4-H and raised a Black Angus steer on my own. In the ninth grade, I decided I wanted out of private school and begged my parents to let me go to public school. They weren't keen on the idea, but I was adamant. When I threatened to run away from home, they came around. On the very first day at my new school, I was sent to the principal's office for dropping a pack of firecrackers down a heating duct in study hall. My parents were livid. But they made me a deal: if I kept a B average through my senior year, they'd let me go to Europe with my best friend, Siggy.

Siggy's mother managed the Chateau Marmont on Sunset Boulevard in Los Angeles. I would spend weekends there at a time when Buddy Hackett, Burl Ives, Eartha Kitt, and Boris Karloff were all living in the hotel. Siggy and I would go to San Fernando drag races and hang out on Sunset Strip and talk about going to Europe, where Siggy's father had decamped with his new wife. When graduation rolled around and I'd kept up my end of the bargain, my parents kept theirs. I sold my two cars for good money, and my Black Angus was auctioned off at the county fair for eighteen hundred dollars. It was a shitload of money for a kid to have in 1961.

The school year barely over, my bags were packed. While my former classmates were primping and priming themselves for senior prom, Siggy and I were getting ready to board a DC-3 propeller airplane for New York City. We stayed with my aunt and uncle in New Jersey, taking the bus to Manhattan every day to visit museums. We went to the Museum of Modern Art, the Guggenheim, the Whitney, the Met, the fucking Museum of Natural History. I couldn't get enough. We went to the Cedar Tavern in Greenwich Village, where I met the painter Franz Kline. After two weeks, my aunt, uncle, and cousins all rode the elevated train with us to the pier, where we boarded an Italian Line ship destined for Europe, the MS *Augustus*. Nine days later, our ocean liner made port in Genoa and our art binge continued. We met Siggy's dad and his wife who took us on the Rapido to their home in San Remo. We made it our base and from there traveled to Spain, France, England, Austria, Germany, Greece. We saw the Louvre, the Tate, all the Gaudí buildings, the Parthenon. Over thirteen months, I took in as much as I could, filling myself up with everything I saw. I also got laid for the very first time. Sometime during that trip it dawned on me: *Oh! I'm not meant to be the world's greatest custom car builder ... I'm an artist!*

Upon my return to the US, I realized I'd outgrown Ojai. I needed to find my own space to work out the epiphany I'd had in Europe. I relocated to Ventura, the nearest big town, where I walked the length of Main Street, the sun beating down, knocking on doors in search of a job. Finally, I came to Danny's Pour House, a tap beer bar. Danny himself asked me if I had any bartending experience. When I mumbled something about having "attended" the bar of an Italian ship, he understood "tended" and I didn't correct him. "Okay, you're hired," he told me. So, at nineteen years old, I worked Saturdays and Sundays pouring beer, a little wine, washing glasses, locking up. I made enough in tips to support myself and spent the rest of the week painting. I'd never painted or drawn anything before, but I found that it wasn't too different from building cars. You just bought materials, transformed them, made something out of nothing.

I moved into a ramshackle Victorian house with a Neanderthal-looking roommate on California Street, near the surf point in Ventura. Another artist lived in the house, a young man named Ken Price. The house was the only structure for miles, a lone grand dame of a home on a four-foot bluff jutting out into the ocean. The only thing separating us from the massive waves was a couple dozen square feet of scraggly old lawn. One day, as I was making a collage out of lacquer and colored tissue paper for the big bay windows overlooking the front porch (to stand in for drapes), Ken and the artist John Altoon walked up.

"Hey! I hear you're artists," I said, tongue in cheek. "What do you think of *my* art?" They made a big show of paying me and my collage little attention. But a few weeks later, Ken told me he was headed to Los Angeles and offered to introduce me to some artists. I went, "Yeah!" He had a beat-up VW with no backseat. I perched in back; his girlfriend, Patty, who was a nurse, sat up front, and Ken drove. Along the way, we stopped at Billy Al Bengston's studio in Venice. I'd never been inside a real artist's studio before. It was a huge space with high ceilings, paintings everywhere. I was blown away. After that, we picked up Judy Henske, the six-foot-tall folk singer, and the two of us drove to West Hollywood crowded in the back of this backseatless car. We ended up at Barney's Beanery, where all Ken's art friends were hanging out in the back room drinking beer. True to his word, he introduced me to Larry Bell, Robert Irwin, Craig Kauffman, Ed Ruscha, Ed Burrell, Dennis Hopper, the art dealer Irving Blum—all emerging figures in the art world at the time. We chatted like equals and I was overtaken with a sense of insppiration. They made me feel as though I, too, could be successful on my own terms as an artist—and have great fun while I was at it. I could feel the world opening up to me. Barney later gave me my very first tab. I wasn't even twenty-one.

Meanwhile, my parents were growing concerned about my life choices. "You're not going to be a lawyer? A doctor?" they fretted. My father's advice was to get a decent job and paint on the weekends. My mom had a better idea: "If you want to be an artist, at least let us send you to art school." (My father, the businessman, had never been happy with my lifestyle. It wasn't until we spent the last three weeks of his life together that he confided how proud he was of me.) I loaded ten paintings I'd made into my 1954 Ford station wagon and drove to the Chouinard Art Institute in Los Angeles. It was summertime and the place was empty save for a receptionist, who told me that admissions were closed to new students. The receptionist's name was Miss Judge, which was fitting given that she saw most of the portfolios that came through the door and had a pretty good idea of what might make the cut. I pulled out a couple of my pieces to show her, wild paintings I'd done in my room in Ventura. White fields with abstract glazed color forms, somewhat reminiscent of Franz Kline and Morris Louis's work. I'd made them by moving colored oil paint mixed with transparent varnish around a blank canvas until the imagery began to emerge, then painted over parts of it with pure white. I asked Miss Judge if she thought they were good enough to apply for the following semester. She took one look at them and phoned the head of painting, the watercolor artist Edward Reep.

The next day, I met with Reep. He leafed through my paintings, looked me square in the face, and offered me a scholarship on the spot. My first class was Introduction to Drawing. I'd never been too engaged in my own education, but I loved art school. Painting, sculpture, art history: it was all so interesting to me. When I wasn't in class or in my makeshift studio (a furnished third-story apartment I promptly unfurnished by throwing all the furniture out the window), I was in the library paging through art books. And for the first time in my academic career, I was a good student. I got almost straight As! It all came so easy.

I was having the time of my life. But art school wasn't the creative Valhalla I'd hoped for. Some of the most progressive artists who taught there—Robert Irwin, Emerson Woelffer, John Altoon—were being pushed out by the conservative Reep. Meanwhile, Walt Disney (and his older brother, Roy) had hatched a plan to merge Chouinard with the Los Angeles Conservatory of Music. The new institution would be called California Institute of the Arts, or CalArts, in the spirit of CalTech. A group of students banded together and rose up against the administration to protest the firing of our best instructors and some of the other changes afoot. I joined them as the junior class representative. When the time came for us to meet with Disney's lawyers, we reserved a long table in the library. Six attorneys, all in gray three-piece suits, showed up. The faculty members stood around the room, their backs leaning up against the walls, arms crossed. One of the suits, a man by the name of John Wesley Dean III, stepped forward. (He would later be known as the White House Counsel for President Richard Nixon in the years leading up to the Watergate scandal.)

"We're very happy that you students have gotten together like this," Dean said. "It shows real initiative. But we have to insist that you put your energy into school dances and art sales."

I stood up, brandishing my middle finger in the direction of the lawyers. "See this?" I said. "Fuck you. This marks the end of my formal education." And I walked out. I sat down on the curb outside the building on the verge of tears. The instructors soon started filing out and surrounded me, offering words of thanks and comfort.

Now, at the age of twenty-three, instead of eight hours in class and eight hours at home painting, which had been my routine for three years, I found myself with sixteen hours a day to make art. But I needed a studio. I rented an old tortilla factory on Temple Street in downtown Los Angeles. It was three hundred feet from the Four Level Interchange, the first major freeway interchange in the world, where the Hollywood and Santa Ana Freeways, the Harbor Freeway, and Arroyo Seco Parkway all converged. The rent was fifteen dollars a month. I shared the space with another artist, divided down the middle with a strip of tape.

CHOUINARD STUDENTS AT THE LEGENDARY HUSSONG'S CANTINA IN ENSENADA, BAJA, WHERE I FIRST TASTED MEZCAL IN 1962. I AM THE ONE WITH MY HEAD ON THE TABLE, PRETENDING TO BE PASSED OUT.

Soon after, I moved to a new space right next door. For thirty bucks a month, I had the whole place to myself. I scavenged windows from Bunker Hill, the highest point in downtown Los Angeles. At the time, it was full of abandoned Victorian houses that were being torn down to make room for new construction. I gathered materials there to build myself a bathroom so that I could live and work out of the same place. And that's been my habit ever since. It's not like I'm a shopkeeper, locking the door and driving home at the end of the day. I'm drawn to large, bright, high-ceilinged spaces where I can both live and work. (I also prefer wide-open bathrooms, furnished with real furniture, like any other room. I've never understood why people keep bathroom doors closed when they're not in use. I guess they fear the scatalogical association. I like a bathroom you can walk around in, where you want to linger.)

Over the next few years, I experimented with different styles and media. I've always enjoyed working with unorthodox materials, like hot-rod lacquer paint and surfboard resin, as well as found art. Ordinary objects, reinterpreted. By the late 1960s, galleries were requesting my pieces for group shows. My first solo exhibition was at Ace Gallery in Los Angeles in 1969. By then, I was working with light, both natural and artificial, in a way that played with people's perceptions. I made these seven- and eight-foot vertical bars of Plexiglass sprayed with up to sixty layers of a transparent lacquer mixed with nacreous pigment for a mother-of-pearl effect. The bars hung on the wall—floating, ever-changing incandescent sculptures. I still get commissions for these pieces today. My early works, along with those of the artists Larry Bell, Robert Irwin, James Turrell, and Doug Wheeler, came to be recognized as part of Southern California's Light and Space Movement.

Around 1972, I started traveling between my studio in Venice, California, and one in New York City. For the next three years, I worked out of a loft space on White Street in Tribeca that had belonged to Barnett Newman, one of the great abstract expressionists. I was given a tab at Max's Kansas City, this legendary bar on Park Avenue South that was frequented by all the cool artists of the day. I spent my nights hanging out with Andy Warhol, Richard Serra, John Chamberlain, Dan Flavin, Michael Heizer, Brice Marden, and Robert Smithson. Life was sweet.

By the early 1980s, Los Angeles was changing. The gentrification of Venice caused anger among longtime residents. It was time to leave. I relocated to Ranchos de Taos, New Mexico, an older part of the greater Taos community. Like Ojai, Taos was a small community with a bohemian vibe and great light and space. It had a large Native American population and strong Hispanic influence. I bought an old trading post to set up as a studio. I was married with a three-year-old daughter at the time, but I don't want to go into the details of that relationship. Suffice it to say that the move led to the end of my marriage. It was a bitter, protracted breakup that left me a very sad man. During this time, I began questioning what I was doing—in my work, on this earth. The artist cliché that suffering fosters creativity was true for me. I witnessed my art change as my life fractured. Anarchy took over as a theme in my pieces. Legal battles over the custody of our child and the division of our property left me depleted and disillusioned. Amid the wreckage, I was faced with a choice: validate my anger in the courtroom or heal. I chose the latter.

I chose Oaxaca. The fuck-you money I'd made that allowed me to go anywhere I wanted for three months was from two big commissions I'd done during the chaos of this painful time. The first was a series of fourteen portrait vases commissioned by Pacific Enterprises that were installed in the company's headquarters on the top floor of the new First Interstate World Center. I used the faces of my friends for the portraits, the silhouettes of their profiles visible in the negative space surrounding each vase. You had to soften your eye to see it. The other piece was a fifteen-foot-high bronze pitcher for IBM. Set on a 45° tilt at Santa Monica Place, it poured three hundred gallons of water per minute into a pool feeding the soul of Los Angeles—a metaphor, but it propelled me to consider filling my own soul.

So, yes, I went back to Oaxaca because a voice inside was telling me I needed to go collaborate with indigenous artisans. I had vivid memories of the hospitality of the Zapotec people and the great art culture there. But I also went to Oaxaca to save myself. I was on a precipice. Oaxaca, the south, the place of soul making, was my salvation. And I leapt in.

THE BIG PITCHER. SANTA MONICA PLACE: IBM AND MCGUIRE THOMAS, 1990.

PORTRAIT OF THE ARTIST AS A YOUNG URN. PRIVATE COLLECTION, 1989.

CHAPTER 2

DIRT ROADS

32

My very first taste of mezcal wasn't in the mountains of Oaxaca. It happened in 1962 at Hussong's Cantina in Ensenada, the oldest and most famous tavern in Baja California. I was the dumb gringo, head tipped back, guzzling right out of the bottle, waiting for the worm to drop into my mouth so I could swallow it. I'd heard it made you trip. The mezcal was harsh, a mouthful of smoke and metal. I woke up terribly hungover the next morning, but that didn't stop me from going right back to the bar the following night. I couldn't forget the strange taste from the night before and ended up trying to drain the bottle again. Mezcal was the first agave spirit I'd ever tasted. I'd never even had tequila.

I wouldn't taste great mezcal—true mezcal—until years later. I traveled to Mexico over the Christmas holiday in 1986 with my wife at the time and Stan and Elyse Grinstein, the godparents of the Los Angeles art world. They had a tradition of inviting a different artist each year to go anywhere they desired. Stan had heard my stories of drinking *pulque*, the fermented maguey drink that predates mezcal, and was intrigued by this ancient elixir. Our wives would not hear of us going alone, so they came with us. We went on an architectural tour of ancient and contemporary masterpieces together. In a taxi going south from Oaxaca City to Mitla, the ancient site of Zapotec and Mixtec rulers, we were stopped at a military checkpoint. A young soldier asked what we were doing in Mexico, and we said we were there to drink pulque. His curiosity piqued, he asked if we'd ever had good mezcal. I replied that I would like to try it. His uncle was bringing some down from the mountains the next day, he said, and he agreed to hold a few liters for me until I could return to claim it. When I tasted it, the world fell away. It smelled of roast agave, had this incredible body, was warming, smoky, savory. It was unlike anything I'd ever tasted. I brought it home to share with my friends, jealously allowing them only small sips so I could make those few liters last.

Four years later, my marriage over, I went to live in Oaxaca for three months to make art. I drove my pickup down from Taos and arrived on a Wednesday. It was the start of spring, the hottest time of year in that part of Mexico. Even back then, parking was terrible—narrow, cobbled roads, cars double-parked. I managed to find a spot a few blocks from where I was staying. The moment I saw my great old friend and the finest weaver in Mexico, Arnulfo Mendoza, he wasted no time inviting me to a fiesta in nearby Teotitlán del Valle.

Arnulfo and I were accompanied by his wife, a Canadian art curator named Mary Jane Gagnier, who had come to Oaxaca as a backpacker and never left, and her friend, a Mexican photographer. Both women were beautiful, and I felt the night's intoxication come on before ingesting a thing. The evening was sultry. We downed

WASHING CLOTHES IN THE RIVER, CHICHICAPA.

dozens of room-temperature Coronitas—miniature Coronas—because there was no refrigeration to speak of. After the third one, they went down like water. We also drank mezcal, of course. At a fiesta, there is always mezcal. Arnulfo and I drank more than our share, stumbled out into the warm night, took a leak, then staggered back into the festivities to dance and drink and laugh some more.

Nowadays, Teotitlán del Valle is a destination for handmade weavings, the main road lined with galleries and shops, even a couple top-notch restaurants. I set up Del Maguey's headquarters here, a village that ignores daylight savings and instead runs on "god's time," which I have to keep in mind when making appointments in other villages. Back in the 1970s, most of the homes in Teotitlán were modest huts with walls made of *carrizo*, a tall bamboo-like reed, and terra-cotta tiles—*tejas*—for roofs. Adobe homes had sprung up here and there, but it would be years before there were any multistoried brick houses around. The road that ran through town was unpaved. There were no sidewalks. There wasn't even a road into Teotitlán from the highway. You had to access it by going through another village, called Macuilxóchitl. Named for the Aztec god of games and dance (and a manifestation of Xochipilli, the Prince of Flowers), Macuilxóchitl sits at the foot of a sacred mountain and is flanked by several small, crumbling pyramids ravaged by cacti and weeds. Its inhabitants harbored a deep enmity against their neighbors in Teotitlán and would charge them an unofficial toll to pass through. Today, it's the people of Macuilxóchitl who are the stonemasons and builders for Teotitlán, now infinitely wealthier than its neighbor, thanks to the popularity of its weavings. The mid-1990s were especially lucrative for Teotitlán. The Southwestern aesthetic was all the rage and everyone from Santa Fe to New York wanted Mexican handwoven textiles.

Master weavers color their own wool with natural dyes. Reds are made with cochineal, a bead-size insect that feeds off the pads of the prickly pear cactus. When dried, its acidic insides can be extracted and mixed with calcium salts to make a red dye known as carmine. (Campari has replaced its colorant with artificial dye, but carmine is making something of a comeback in everything from food coloring to lipstick as manufacturers return to natural ingredients.) Blues can be made from indigo, a flowering plant distantly related to green peas, yellows from dried marigolds, browns from crushed pecan shells. Mesoamerican people have used these natural colorants since ancient times. When the Spaniards arrived, they were astounded by the deep reds woven into the colorful textiles worn by the natives. In Europe, red was an expensive color to manufacture, a symbol of wealth and aristocracy. Even in Renaissance paintings, it was said that no true red existed—at least not for long. The richness of red paint would soon fade. The Spanish began importing

WILD *MAGUEY* GROWING IN THE COUNTRYSIDE.

cochineal, keeping their source a secret and prohibiting its export from Mexico to other countries. For centuries, the rest of Europe was forced to rely on Spain as the gatekeeper of cochineal. The red dye it produced was proclaimed the first true red and became a more valuable export than all the gold, jewels, and silver the conquest extracted from Mexico.

Cochineal is used to make a range of red tones. Mix it with soda ash to make purple, citric acid for orange. Playing with pH levels to make new colors is an art in itself. But before you can dye anything, you need wool. The weavers of Teotitlán had several sources for wool, and the village of Chichicapa was considered one of the best. Located some forty miles away, it's separated from the Central Valley of Oaxaca by a mountain range running along the Pan-American Highway. To get there from Teotitlán, you have to go around the mountains, a three-hour drive at least. I made the trek with my friend, Pancho (the same Pancho I would later smuggle across the US border), and two of his brothers, Sergio and Mito. We woke in the middle of the night and set off at three in the morning. Their parents were terrified, pleading with us to reconsider the trip.

"They kill people there," they said.

I was baffled by their fear; there was nothing to back it up. But I soon came to understand the insular and superstitious nature of the people of Teotitlán. They did not travel—not for pleasure, anyway. They might take their wares to markets in the city, but rarely did they venture out for the sake of discovery. They were afraid of the unknown. And, for them, the unknown began at the threshold of their own village and stretched out into the infinite beyond.

Luckily, Pancho and his brothers had a spark of the adventurous in them. We took their VW van, rolling out into the quiet night. The drive was slow going, as it always is on Oaxaca's rough roads, but especially so in the dark. We arrived in Chichicapa shortly after dawn. The sound the van made when it pulled into the village—the *tucka-tucka-tucka* of the engine, the crunching of tires on dirt—announced our arrival. It was the only vehicle in town. Women with white-streaked hair pulled back into neat buns or long braids coiled on top of their heads emerged from their humble adobe homes. They knew exactly why we'd come. Their outstretched hands held five-inch balls of yarn, spun from wool shorn from the sheep they kept. We rolled through the village buying wool from every woman we saw, filling the back of the van.

When no more would fit, we started sniffing out a place to eat. We were hungry and cold after the long drive through the mountains in an unheated van. There were no restaurants in Chichicapa or in any of the villages I traveled to back then. If you happened to be passing through, a woman would welcome you into her home and cook for you in exchange for a small fee. Before finding food, Pancho suggested we hunt down some mezcal, which the brothers often did when they arrived in Chichicapa early in the morning. We picked our way up a ravine next to a stream, which is where you go to find mezcal if any is to be found. A palenque should always be located next to a pristine water source. Next to the stream, we found several men with pitchforks and shovels digging into what looked like a mound of dirt. It was a maguey roast. Once uncovered, the caramelized piñas came out steaming, filling the air with the smell of cooked pumpkin and burnt sugar. A man with a slight stature and angular jawline appeared to be in charge. Pancho, his brothers, and I introduced ourselves and asked if he had any mezcal to sell. His name was Faustino García Vásquez. He was the poorest man in the village, I later learned, but he made the best mezcal. He had no palenque of his own, but rented that of a neighbor to make his mezcal. Uncapping a jerrycan, he poured some into a jícara, the dried, hollow gourd used as a bowl or cup. The mezcal was like nothing I'd ever tasted. Other than what I'd bought in 1986, all the mezcal I'd had until that point was spiked with chemicals and god-knows-what. This was pure.

ME WITH DON COSME MARTÍNEZ (LEFT) AND DON BETO HERNANDEZ (RIGHT).

HOW
MEZCAL IS
MADE

FAUSTINO GARCÍA VÁSQUEZ, CHICHICAPA.

THE HARVEST

Mezcal is the crystal-clear liquid distilled from the agave or *maguey* plant. The large, spiky plants are harvested, their spiny leaves sliced off with a machete, to reveal the heart of the plant, which is known as the *piña*. The hearts are transported to the *palenque*, the rustic distillery where mezcal is made.

MARCOS CRUZ MENDEZ, SAN LUIS DEL RÍO.

THE ROAST

The piñas, halved or quartered, are loaded into a *horno*. At this point, the earthen oven has already been heated using some variety of slow-burning wood, like black oak, for some five hours. The maguey is arranged over the red-hot rocks from the fire in a mound, the piñas layered like fruit slices in a deep-dish pie crust. The mound, as much as ten feet wide and ten feet high, is covered with spent maguey fibers, called *bagazo*, and earth to trap the heat inside. A roast usually lasts four or five days, but can last much longer, depending on the maguey variety. When it's complete, the piñas, brown and caramelized, are uncovered.

PREPARING THE ROAST, SAN LUIS DEL RÍO.

THE CRUSH

The roasted maguey is ground in one of several ways. It can be transferred to a *molino* (mill), a stone pit with a one-ton stone wheel affixed to the center of it. An animal, usually a horse, is hitched up to the wheel and slowly walked around and around the pit, as the wheel crushes the maguey inside. Alternatively, the roasted maguey is placed in a trough or hollowed-out tree trunk where it is mashed by hand using a large mallet or club.

GRINDING MAGUEY BY HAND, SANTA CATARIA MINAS.

FERMENTATION

The juices, meats, and fibers of the maguey are collected from the molino and transferred to wooden fermentation vats, called *tinas*. Fermentation occurs naturally, with the help of ambient yeasts and other airborne microbes living in the palenque, embedded in the walls of the tinas, and on the skins of the maguey themselves. These microorganisms feed off the sugar in the maguey mash, a process that produces alcohol and carbon dioxide, the latter of which gets released into the air. Depending on the weather—cooler temperatures will lead to a slower fermentation, while warmer temperatures will encourage a quicker one—fermentation can last for several days to several weeks. (Mezcal can be made year-round except for when it's very rainy.) A few days in, a dose of local spring water is added to the ferment to give the yeasts and microbes more space to reproduce. The mixture bubbles and hisses, emitting warm, sweet aromas, until fermentation is complete.

GATHERING AROUND THE FERMENTATION TANKS, SANTA CATARINA MINAS.

DISTILLATION

The fermented maguey juice, along with the fibers, is fed into pot stills. These are usually made of copper, a material known to leach impurities from alcoholic vapors during distillation. The still is affixed to an adobe oven that houses a roaring wood fire. As the mixture heats up and reaches its boiling point, it gives off vapors that rise. The vapors are collected in the condenser, a copper tube cooled with water, which turns the vapors to liquid. The most traditional stills are made of clay with bamboo-like tubing, called *carrizo*. In this ancient style of still, a copper bowl sits in the mouth of the pot and is filled with cold water. As the vapors rise, they reach the base of the bowl, where they are collected and condensed. The condensed vapors then drip into the bamboo tubing and are collected at the other end. Distillation is typically carried out twice.

The first part of the distillate is known as the *puntas*, or heads, made up of volatile alcohols. The last part of the distillate, which contains methanol, is known as the *colas*, or tails. The middle part is the heart: *el corazón*. This is what the distiller wants to cut out and use. The first distillation run produces *ordinario*, a weak alcohol clocking in at maybe 40 proof. By law, the distiller must distill the ordinario a second time, blending the appropriate parts—heads, tails, and heart—to make mezcal. Traditionally, mezcal is not aged in barrels, but may be aged in glass.

CLAY POT DISTILLATION, SANTA CATARINA MINAS

I stood by the stream, hearing the rush of water over rocks as the spirit slid down my throat and into my belly. My feet lifted an eighth of an inch off the ground. I'd been tired, but half an ounce jolted me back to life. A happy high. And the flavor—it was like a light being turned on. I felt like I was tasting everything around me—the earth beneath my feet, the rushing water, the slick rocks, the cold morning air, the mountains, the sky. It was as though layers were being peeled away from my mind like onion skins. I was transformed.

I looked over at my amigos and saw in their eyes that they were right there with me. We were happy. No one spoke. We just watched the men as they uncovered the roast. There were probably twelve tons of maguey hearts in the pit, enough to make more than a thousand liters of mezcal. Using pitchforks, the men removed the coarse hairlike fibers called *bagazo* under which the piñas had been buried. The roast was covered with *petates*, woven palm mats used as bedrolls, to trap the heat inside. There are producers who use fan palm leaves; others use banana leaves, which might impart a tropical aroma. Every part of the process, from the type of firewood to the blanketing layer affect the final result. Roasting over mesquite wood, for example, may give you an overly smoked mezcal. Black oak will be more earthy and subtle. Everything the palenqueros do is intentional, practical.

I returned to Teotitlán with yarn for my weavings and the taste of mezcal in my mouth. It stuck with me the way a painting or a photograph does. I recognized it as art, plain and simple. And I wanted more. I wanted to use it in my art, add it to my array of unorthodox media. Use it to fill one of my vessels—or, more accurately, construct a vessel worthy of holding it. This is when I dreamed up the idea of the Ometochtli portrait bottle filled with the best mezcal I could find. (Ometochtli actually represents an infinite multitude of gods and goddesses associated with intoxication and ecstasy from pulque, the fermented beer-like beverage made from the sap of certain maguey varieties. These deities include the Centzon Totochin, or Four Hundred Rabbits, said to represent the myriad manifestations of euphoria. The Greco-Roman tradition has Bacchus, god of wine and religious ecstasy, but the Aztecs had a god or goddess for each of the varied moments of rhapsody—the touch of a lover, the smell of a flower, the "aha" of an idea. My dealer at the time suggested that the piece comprise a room with four hundred bottles.)

I began venturing out every third day in search of the spirit. One day for art, one day for culture, and the third for mezcal. But good mezcal is never easy to get to. The famed Pan-American Highway that had first led me to Oaxaca in 1970 is partly to blame. When it was built in 1950, it opened the door to cheap *aguardiente*—firewater—from Guatemala, which soon flooded Oaxaca. Mezcal makers found it hard to compete in the local markets without adulterating their spirit somehow. Mezcal, made from plants that can take a generation to grow, is expensive to produce. By the time I started my search, whatever mezcal was readily available in the city or in major markets was watered-down, chemically cut shit with food coloring, flavoring, and a worm in the bottom. City Oaxacans drank it because most of them had migrated from their villages for economic reasons and had forgotten anything else existed. True mezcal did exist, only it was hidden deep in the mountains—in a state of grace, unchanged for centuries.

I've continued to produce and exhibit works related to the effects of the infinite gods and goddesses of intoxication and ecstasy. On May Day 2015, I had a show in Taos of works spanning twenty-five years, comprised of flattened plastic bottles found on the road between Pancho's house and my own, painted with *dichos*, adages taken from the culture down there. The bottles had been trampled by thousands of grazing goats, dump trucks, kids on bicycles, and barefoot women on their way to the market. Their sculptural forms and transparency inspired me.

I never finished my Ometochtli art project. After making just one maquette of the blue glass portrait bottle, my attention shifted to the liquid inside. Of the twenty-eight samples of mezcal I collected from around the region during those three months in Oaxaca, I never decided which was the best, which would be the one to fill the vessel. I recognized that each was its own work of art. When my time in Oaxaca was up and I drove back to Taos with my pickup piled high with art, Pancho hidden behind the driver's seat, and a five-gallon jug of wedding mezcal sitting on the side of the bed, those twenty-eight samples of mezcal were with me, too. Buried among the weavings, pottery, sculpture, and furniture I brought back to the US were the treasures that I still had no idea would become the seeds of Del Maguey.

THE PROTOTYPE FOR MY
OMETOCHTLI PORTRAIT BOTTLE.

HERDING LIVESTOCK IN FRONT OF THE *PALENQUE*, CHICHICAPA.

DEL MAGUEY CHICHICAPA

SINGLE VILLAGE MEZCAL

The village of Chichicapa sits in a broad desert valley at some 5,000 feet in elevation. A patchwork of tropical microclimates surrounding it offers tremendous biodiversity. Chichicapa is often characterized as the smokiest of the Del Maguey Single Village Mezcals. I'm not sure I agree. It was the first mezcal we ever released—and is often the first great mezcal people taste—so perhaps the smoke registers more significantly simply because it's a new flavor to many people. To me, this mezcal is intricate and sinewy, like the musculature of a dancer. It shows plenty of citrus notes and a refreshing hint of mint at the finish.

Production Notes

VILLAGE: San Balthazar Chichicapa

PALENQUEROS: Faustino García Vásquez and Maximino García Chávez

STATE: Oaxaca

REGION: Valles Centrales

MAGUEY: Espadín (*Agave angustifolia* Haw.)

AGE OF MAGUEY: 7–8 years

ELEVATION: 5,052 feet (1540 meters)

ROAST DURATION: 4–5 days

TYPE OF WOOD: Oak, eucalyptus, huamúchil, ocote, sabino

MILLING: Wheel

SIZE OF TINAS: 1700 L

FERMENTATION DURATION: 6–8 days

WATER SOURCE: Well

STILL TYPE: Copper

STILL SIZE: 350 L

VOL ORDINARIO PER TINA: 300–350 L

ABV OF MEZCAL: 46%

VOL MEZCAL PRODUCED PER TINA: 150–180 L

CHAPTER 3

SEEDS

At my first studio in Taos, the old trading post, my good friend Dennis Hopper and the actor Dean Stockwell paid me a visit. Right next to the front door was an old mesquite table where the book *The Death Ship* sat. The story, originally published in German by B. Traven (a pseudonym), is about a drunken sailor lost in post–World War I Europe. He has no passport or proof of identity, so he just keeps getting deported from country to country, until finally he lands on this skeletal ship manned by other nameless, paperless souls. Basically, the guy gets fucked because of bureaucracy. Dennis Hopper and Dean Stockwell each put a hand on the book. They didn't read it, but just by touching it they knew they wanted to make a movie about *The Death Ship*. And that's how I learned you can put your hand on something and know what it's about. It's like this piece in my kitchen in Oaxaca. David Byrne gave me a book sealed in plastic on the shamans of the Mixteca. I never opened it, but instead drove holes through it, bolting it to a corrugated tin panel, and hung it on the wall. When I put my hand on it, I knew what was inside.

Over the three months I worked and lived in Oaxaca in 1990, I believed I was gathering samples of mezcal to use in an art project. I always knew, the moment I met the producer of the mezcal or saw where it was made, that it would be special. Tasting it only confirmed what I could see in the face of the palenquero or smell in the air of the palenque. I can't explain it: it was my *don*, my gift, to find myself in the presence of great mezcal, to have mezcal find me. Once I'd smuggled the twenty-eight samples—and Pancho—safely across the border, I knew these liquid works of art were meant to be shared. Among the samples was the mezcal from Chichicapa made by Faustino García Vásquez. I didn't know it at the time, but he would become the first collaborator in my new project.

After the episode at the border, when I was forced to dump three of my five gallons of wedding mezcal down the drain, I made a decision. I would find a way to bring mezcal into the country legally. Unsure of how to go about it, I tapped one of the only people in the liquor business I knew. I'd met Steve Wallace, of the landmark wine shop Wally's Wine & Spirits in Los Angeles, years before through art friends. He'd taught me a few things about good wine back then, when having money in my pocket was new to me and I was still figuring out how I wanted to spend it. I invited Wallace to come taste through the twenty-eight samples with me. He was fascinated. When I told him of my plan to start some sort of company to bring mezcal into the country, he introduced me to Carl Doumani, the founder of Stags' Leap Winery, in Napa. Carl spent a few days with me in Taos. We tasted each mezcal. He became so enamored with the spirit that he offered to be my partner. He would give me 100 percent of the money needed to get my company, Del Maguey, off the ground and we would split the profits fifty-fifty.

"All you have to do," he told me, "is pour these four village samples into one bottle to make a blend. Oh, and get rid of those woven baskets the bottles come in." Blending was the only way to make a product consistent, he said. And the woven baskets were just too kitschy. I didn't know much about mezcal just yet, but I knew that mixing the villages was tantamount to sacrilege. Each mezcal was not just *from* a distinct village; it *was* the village. It was the aroma and flavor of each singular place, distilled. More importantly, it was the hand of each maker—his unique touch that communicated his years of experience, his style, his technique, his sensibility, his family history, his pain, his joy—bottled. As an artist, I understood each sample as a distinct piece of work and wasn't about to violate the work's integrity. I turned Carl down.

Instead, I went about getting an import license and forming a company on my own. The World Wide Web was still uncharted territory, but I registered the domain name www.mezcal.com. (I kept it until, years later, the mezcal regulatory board asked if they could use it.) I had friends who wanted to invest in Del Maguey, not in the company as a whole but in specific villages, which allowed them to get in for little money and gave me enough to get going. For as little as $5,000, a friend could buy into his favorite mezcal, the funds going toward the village of his choice and, ideally, earn a tidy return when that village's mezcal finally started turning a profit. My vision for the enterprise hadn't quite solidified when the recession hit in 1990. Skittish about starting a new business during an economic downturn, I put my plans on hold. For the next five years, I busied myself making art, traveling to Oaxaca when I could, and contemplating the best way to bring mezcal to the world.

Oaxaca was still largely untouched by the outside world. Exporting mezcal was beyond the realm of people's imaginations back then. I didn't discuss it much, but kept returning to the four villages I wanted to work with. I was slowly getting to know these families, and they were getting to know me. They kept making their spirit as they always had. They didn't quite understand my intentions yet, but they always welcomed me. On one trip back to Mexico, I went to see Faustino and shared with him my plan to export mezcal to the United States. I told him I wanted him to be a part of my venture. I won't say he didn't believe me—he took the news as he takes everything, with practiced quietude—but I suspect the idea was so far-fetched that he didn't place much stock in it.

As the economy slowly bounced back, I began to feel the time was right to launch Del Maguey. I went to see Faustino. This time, I struck a deal with him to produce a three-hundred-liter batch of mezcal. It was a number I pulled out of thin air, having no clue about the liquor business, but it was an order he said he could fill. He had no palenque of his own; he made his mezcal in a rented still. I offered to build him a palenque on a rangy patch of land he had at the edge of town. He was over the moon. With my investment, he was able to pay for materials and hire his friends to help construct a palenque. When it was done, he was so proud to show off how he'd laid it out, even the little area he'd set up for lounging and resting. Long hours are spent stoking the stills; a man needs a place to lay his head.

Two months after the palenque was completed, the first batch was ready. It usually takes a while to break in a new still, but the first batches Faustino made came out great. I arranged to go pick up my three hundred liters. To transport the mezcal from Chichicapa, I had ordered two hundred used fifty-six-liter stainless steel beer barrels from San Antonio, Texas—Pearl and Pabst Blue Ribbon barrels because they were cheap. When I got to Faustino's, we had a taste of his mezcal and immediately I knew something was wrong.

"What the fuck?!" I exclaimed. The mezcal was astringent, green in an unripe way. It tasted nothing like the Chichicapa I'd come to know and love. "*Cálmate, cálmate,*" Faustino reassured me. "It's only three days old. It's like a newborn

FAUSTINO ON OUR FIRST BOTTLE LABEL IN 1995.

MAXIMINO AND ISABEL'S WEDDING, 2012.

baby. It takes a couple weeks to settle." It was true. A couple weeks later, it was the Chichicapa I'd tasted up by the stream years before. And that's how I learned to trust the hand of the maker. No matter what Faustino makes, it's always going to be Chichicapa: rich and muscular, yet graceful, with a lifted minty note at the end. I also learned how to taste mezcal through interpolation. Just as a winemaker can imagine what a wine will taste like by sampling the grapes, seasoned mezcal makers can taste a new mezcal and foresee what it will be once it's ready. It was a great lesson.

I would learn many more lessons working with Faustino. In 1995, there was no certification required, no regulations surrounding mezcal production. It was so beautifully simple. There we were, producing this pure spirit out in the open air, happy as can be. We would sit together and sip mezcal, smoking Camels, exchanging few words, but somehow cultivating a deep friendship. It was a very masculine bond. Faustino was a handsome man back then and still is, though weatherworn. He looked like a Mexican Marlboro man with his jet-black hair and thick mustache, his rough brown hands raising the burning butt of an unfiltered cigarette to his mouth. He carried a big dagger on his hip, as farmers in hill country do, for slicing off a chunk of roast agave to sample, or a bunch of bananas off a tree, or to hack a path through a brambly field. Even in Zapotec, he spoke little. And yet, he was not suspicious of me as many Zapotecs were. Rather, he seemed to be always hanging back, looking out through his eyes at me, just watching. He was a wise dude. He let me be the animated gringo that I am. But, being around him, quiet as he was, I learned to use fewer words, too. It served me well with the other palenqueros, not being so effusive. They didn't respond well to chatter. In time, I adopted Faustino's calm and watchfulness as my own.

Today, Faustino is still quiet and watchful. And those hands—permanently stained from tobacco and maguey, the bulging flesh of his palms always split from some farming accident or another. He has a son, Maximino, to whom he is passing the torch. Like his father, Maximino is a man of few words. Handsome like his father, though taller and fuller in his face and build, he is becoming a great distiller, too. I was named the godfather at his wedding, a sacred role that essentially ties me to the family for life. Not long ago, Maximino threw his father a surprise party for his fifty-seventh birthday. When I walked in, Faustino beamed. Seven whole lambs had been buried underground and roasted for hours. Minutes after they were uncovered and steaming hunks of meat distributed to those hovering by the cook, the belly and innards were chopped up and stirred into a bright red broth. The soup was served with raw shredded cabbage and cilantro for heaping into the center of the bowl. The meal revived those who had been celebrating for several hours already. Faustino and I took many

FAUSTINO GARCÍA VÁSQUEZ IN HIS PRISTINE
PALENQUE IN CHICHICAPA.

toasts together that afternoon. Each one was ceremonial, looking into each other's eyes as we raised our copitas.

Several men from the village showed up for the party, the same men who usually hang around for distillation. They aren't officially employees of Faustino's, but they play an important role, sleeping next to the still and stoking the fires overnight. He pays them in mezcal. The fruit flies that inevitably swarm an open bottle of mezcal are known as *borrachos*: drunks. Real borrachos, drawn to the palenque like flies, are said to be good luck during distillation. The more of them around, the better the batch will be. So goes the lore. Come fiesta time, they expect to reap their rewards.

Gabe Bonfanti, our head of sustainability, is a husky, bearded, and jovial Taos-born genius who played professional baseball in Italy. His role at Del Maguey is to find solutions for the everyday problems that arise in the villages we work with, from building bridges over rivers to digging wells and installing cell phone towers. For Faustino's party, he hired a mariachi band from the next village over. (I got my old friend a new mouth: he'd ground his teeth down and his wife, Sabrina, had grown worried he'd no longer be able to eat her cooking.) The men drank and danced, and one of them snoozed at the feet of his friends on the ground. The women took breaks from cooking and serving to dance, too. I spent the afternoon dancing under the hot sun with the *viejas*, kicking up dust as we moved. Faustino let loose. For him, this meant swaying quietly among the mariachis, bumping into them gently when he lost his footing, his watchful eyes shining beneath the wide brim of his black cowboy hat.

My first shipment of mezcal landed in Albuquerque on December 16, 1995. It contained fifty-four cases of mezcal from Chichicapa and another village, San Luis del Río. The US Customs agents, who had helped me for months, answering my questions on how to import, cheered as it came through. Shipments from two other villages, Santa Catarina Minas and Santo Domingo Albarradas, followed in 1996. The bottles were encased in woven covers, similar to ones I'd found in the Mercado Benito Juárez, in Oaxaca, to cover many of the sample bottles that traveled incognito with me and Pancho across the border. My friend, the photographer Rusty Reniers, was an early seed investor in Del Maguey and had agreed to take charge of imports and sales while I traveled back and forth to Oaxaca. He picked up the first shipment and immediately ran a case over to Mark Miller at the Coyote Cafe in Santa Fe. We were in business.

Progressive chefs like Mark Miller instantly embraced the spirit. But, in 1995, progressive chefs were few and far between. Most people were skittish about trying mezcal. The United States was in the grips of the tequila boom, and there didn't seem to be much room in the collective imagination for another agave spirit from Mexico—certainly not one with ties to ancient, sacred customs that was meant to be sipped neat and not shot back with lime and salt. I remember taking bottles to restaurants and bars for the owner or manager to try. I was met with skepticism, even revulsion. There were establishments where no one was brave or curious enough to even taste my mezcal. Instead, they would summon the dishwasher from the kitchen and order him to taste it. "You're Mexican," they'd say. "You try it." But little by little, one person at a time, face-to-face and nose-to-nose, I began to convert people.

Some people needed no convincing. Jimmy Yeager, of Jimmy's in Aspen, was an early fan. He introduced me to Steve Olson, a cocktail consultant who spent much of his time preaching about tequila. He gave seminars on tequila, trying to get people to understand that it was a cultural product with history and pedigree. One day, Steve and Jimmy invited me down to Santa Fe, where Steve was hosting the first Grand Margarita cocktail competition, sponsored by Grand Marnier. I walked into a space across from Coyote Cafe, where the contest was being held, expecting to go unnoticed. Steve, orating from the front of the room, stopped midspeech.

"And this must be Ron Cooper!" he called out. All eyes were on me. I'd never been introduced to a large group of bartenders before. I wondered, in that moment, what exactly this man wanted with me and what he'd told the room about me before I walked in. It was at once reassuring and perplexing to find people so interested in what I was doing.

That evening, Jimmy, Steve, and I hung out at the Coyote Cafe with the chef Mark Miller, Grand Marnier heiress Alexandra Marnier Lapostolle, and Robert Denton, the importer of Chinaco and El Tesoro, the first truly great tequilas to enter the United States. Mark's cocktail, The Smokin' Margarita, had won second place in the competition and would become Del Maguey's signature cocktail for many years to come. Steve and I went back to his hotel room and stayed up all night talking agave spirits. We came to the conclusion that we both wanted nothing more in this world than to bring mezcal to it. Steve had the ear of the restaurant and bar community. In the following years, first chefs and then mixologists would provide the gateway to mezcal. Cocktails became people's initiation into the spirit. Steve offered his expertise without asking for any payment in return. I ended up crashing on his bed that night. I was too poor to rent my own room and too drunk to drive back up to Taos.

The first big contract between Faustino and Del Maguey stipulated that he would make twenty-four hundred liters of mezcal for us. I had the same agreement with the three other villages I started with. It took them each about a year to make that much mezcal and it would take me years more to sell it all. Rusty, in the meantime, was splitting his time between his photography career and working for Del Maguey. A redheaded firebrand I'd met through a mutual friend, he was invaluable to me then and I was loath to lose his help, but it soon became clear that he wasn't the right person for the job. He admitted as much to me over the phone one day while I was in Oaxaca. It was a sweltering spring morning and I hung up the phone sweating, as much out of anxiety over Del Maguey's future as because of the heat. Before letting myself spiral into a panic, I called an old friend, Michael Gardner, whom I'd known since he was eight years old. He was the son of a couple who'd collected my art for years. Tall and broad, with a surfer's build and a flop of reddish-blond hair, he grew up in Trancas Beach, Malibu, around the artists his parents supported. I was still a kid myself when we met, maybe twenty-four years old. I remember chasing him around the house, giving him shit like an older brother would. I built him his first skateboard and, years later, he came to ski in Taos and helped me finish building a 1978 Cadillac Coupe de Ville that I planned to drive to Mexico. Michael was a real surf brat at heart, but he followed in his father and grandfather's footsteps and went to business school. He also studied poetry. He was a rare breed, with full command of both his left and his right brain.

At the time, Michael was the head of institutional investment for Bank of America in Santa Monica. The bank was moving his department to San Francisco, and Michael was offered the option of relocating or resigning with six months' severance pay. He took the severance package and rented a house two blocks from the beach, where he intended to spend the next six months writing poetry.

"How would you like to be the head of sales for Del Maguey?" I asked him.

"No fucking way," he said. After a pause, he added, "It's Friday. I'll take until Monday to think about it." Fifteen minutes later, he called back and agreed to take the job, rattling off a list of conditions. His poetry would have to wait.

Michael had already visited me in Taos and Oaxaca many times and developed a deep appreciation for mezcal. But he knew nothing about the liquor industry. He used his business acumen to figure out how to proceed, but learned the trade largely through trial and error. I never worried about him. Michael was bright. But more importantly, I believed he understood what I was trying to do. He saw that it was an art project as much as it was a company. Like me, he was fascinated by the different taste profiles produced by each village, even though they all used the same variety of maguey—espadín—and almost identical production practices. Michael was the one who coined the term "Single Village Mezcal." It helped people understand the spirit in familiar wine terms. All four villages made mezcal from the same raw material using the same method, yet each mezcal was unique to its place.

I met Michael a couple weeks later in Mexico City. We drove to Oaxaca in a brand-new Ford Lobo, a style of pickup that was new in Mexico. It had a modern engine and suspension, four-wheel drive, and an extra backseat. Once we were out of the city, we stopped by the side of the road and bought fresh coconuts to drink in the sunshine. Out on the road, we saw a sign for Tlaxcala. I'd heard of a pulque producer there, so we decided to take the exit. Fresh pulque is nothing like what you find in the *pulquerías* of Mexico City, where jars of stale liquid are flavored with fruit juice. The fermented maguey drink, a sort of milky beer with a gentle effervescence, is best consumed within days of production. Like mezcal, pulque has sacred roots. Both the Aztecs and the Mayas used it in religious ceremonies. Notably, public drunkenness was not tolerated by the Aztecs. It was punishable by death. But pulque was prescribed for the sick, the elderly, and pregnant women. Its ritual use could grant you access to the gods.

We drove through the center of Tlaxcala, past a quaint colonial plaza, and down a narrow road shaded by eucalyptus trees. We came upon a little store and pulled over to ask if there was any pulque for sale. To our surprise, a woman rushed out, yelling, "He's in the shower! He'll be right out!" In moments, her husband emerged and jumped into the backseat of our truck. Without asking us who we were or what we wanted, he started guiding us down one dirt road, then another, to the rustic brewery, called a *tinacal*, where he made pulque. The air in the tinacal was funky and warm. It smelled of fresh-baked sourdough bread.

It turned out the pulque maker thought I was the Tlaxcala governor's helicopter pilot there to pick up a batch. We set him straight, telling him we were just a couple of gringos looking for pulque, which seemed to amuse him. He showed us around, pointing out two rows of maguey he'd planted, one male and one female. The plants were enormous, about twelve feet in diameter and nine feet tall, like granddaddies of the maguey I was accustomed to seeing in Oaxaca. He scooped raw sap, known

as *aguamiel*—honey water—from the heart of one of the plants for us to taste.
Nearby, an open vat filled with mother seed, like the starter for sourdough, foamed
and gurgled, alive with native yeasts and other microorganisms. The pulque maker
removed the top from another vat and a huge cloud of fruit flies whooshed out. There
would be no health inspector coming around these parts. He filled a couple jícaras
with fresh pulque. It was silky and tangy with a gentle prickle on the tongue. As we
gulped it down, our eyes grew slitty. The colors around us brightened, the drone of
flies buzzing up near the ceiling intensified. A sort of psychedelic haze engulfed us.
Each knew what the other was thinking before he spoke and burst into giggles at
jokes before they were told out loud. The pulque maker began to reveal how the elixir
had saved him. He couldn't have kids until he started drinking it, he told us. Pulque
made him fertile and strong, like an ox.

When we got back to Oaxaca, Michael, Pancho, and I celebrated Michael's new
role at Del Maguey with a little too much mezcal. Michael had already been drinking
pulque for hours, so he promptly passed out. Years later, he told me about a dream he
had that night. It remained as vivid in his memory as the moment he'd woken from it.

In the dream, he was in a beautiful place, looking out over a sacred mountain, not
unlike the one in Macuilxóchitl. He tilted his head back and opened his mouth. A herd
of moths burst forth from his open lips with the force of a tornado. The moth cloud
spiraled up and arced, then hurtled itself into the top of the sacred mountain. Michael
is still able to close his eyes and see the dream, feel the downy wings of the moths
beating in his cheeks. A flock of moths is called an *eclipse*. These night-flying brethren
of butterflies are closely linked to maguey: the plant invites these pollinators to feast
on its flowers after dark. Michael, who is now the CEO of Del Maguey, knew nothing
of moths pollinating maguey at the time. He's always wondered if the mezcal itself
was speaking to him from inside his own body. There's much to be said about the
effects mezcal has on the body and brain, although it's all speculative. No one knows
for sure how it cracks opens the mind or why it energizes rather than depresses, as
other forms of alcohol do. There's a reason it's used in sacred rituals, as pulque once
was. I don't wish to perpetuate the myth that mezcal makes you trip. But I do believe
that good, organic mezcal can help unlock certain mysteries that dwell within us. Can
it reverse infertility? Bring you closer to god? Honestly, I don't doubt it.

WHAT IS PULQUE?

Pulque might be described as the precursor to mezcal, the way beer is the precursor to whiskey. It's a beverage fermented from the sap of the *maguey* that dates back to the Aztec Empire and the Mayas before them. Unfortunately, little is known of Mayan culture, but we do have insights into how pulque was consumed by the Aztecs. Pulque was taken as a ceremonial drink, as well as for curative purposes. Recreational consumption of pulque was prohibited. Priests and shamans drank it as a way to communicate with the gods. On such holy days as Day of the Dead, pulque could be enjoyed by all.

The magueys used to make pulque are enormous plants, and are mostly found in central Mexico. The plant's sap is scraped from its heart not once but repeatedly for several months until the plant runs dry. The collected sap is taken to the *tinacal*, or brewery, and placed in fermentation tanks (*tinas*). The sap is mixed with water and left to ferment naturally with the help of ambient yeasts and bacteria. The result is a milky, tangy, and slightly effervescent beverage that rarely contains more than 5 percent alcohol.

After the end of the Aztec era, pulque's sacred status dwindled. Public consumption rose. Pulque became associated with poor, indigenous, and mestizo communities. To the Spanish, it was foul and eventually banned. But the Spanish Crown soon realized that a better solution would be to tax it. By the eighteenth century, taxes collected from the sale of pulque accounted for the greatest slice of government revenue in Mexico.

Today, several old *pulquerías* in Mexico City survive and a number of new ones have opened, but they mostly sell pulque infused with fruit flavors. Authentic pulque is best enjoyed unadulterated and fresh, within days of production, when it's tart and refreshing, with bright citrus aromas and a gentle fizz.

A GUIDE TO MAGUEY

The maguey plant looks prehistoric. In fact, it can be traced to the Cenozoic era, just after dinosaurs went extinct. More than two hundred varieties of maguey—widely known by its Latin name, *agave*—exist, and the vast majority of them are native to Mexico. Perhaps the best-known variety is Blue Weber agave, or *Agave tequilana*, the type used to make tequila. Before blue agave became a household name, the most recognizable type of agave was probably *henequén*, a species farmed in the Yucatan and used in the production of rope for ships until DuPont invented the synthetic fabric nylon in 1935. In time, the demand for henequén fell and many agave farms were abandoned.

In Oaxaca, the most common maguey species is espadín, named for its long, green sword-shaped leaves. (Espadín comes from *espada*, Spanish for "sword.") It is the genetic ancestor of blue agave and, like its progeny, takes an average of seven years to reach maturity. Of course, much depends on the climate and soil in which the maguey grows. In some villages with heavier rainfall and a more humid microclimate, maguey can ripen faster. In others that are drier and sunnier, it matures more slowly.

While espadín is generally farmed, it also grows in the wild. Wild agave propagates sexually, while farmed agave is propagated asexually. When left to propagate sexually, an agave plant grows a *quiote*, or long stalk, from its heart that can grow to reach twenty feet high. From the top sprout tiny flowers that are pollinated by a motley cast of birds, insects, and bats. The flowers produce seeds, which scatter to produce new plants. When a plant is propagated asexually, its quiote is cut to concentrate all its energy on developing sugars in the heart. After a few years, a plant begins to produce offshoots, known as *hijuelos*. These offshoots, which grow out from the mother plant, are cut off and replanted in groves. (You sometimes hear of "semiwild" agave, which usually refers to plants that have been grown from seeds that were collected in the wild and planted by hand.) Of the hundreds of varieties of maguey, about thirty can be used to make mezcal.

MORE ON MAGUEY

In Oaxaca, wild maguey species go by names such as tobalá, madrecuixe, tobasiche, barril, arroqueño, tepextate, and papalome. Each one can be identified by its physical characteristics and each has typical flavor characteristics, but what dictates the taste of mezcal above all is the environment in which the maguey grows and the hand of the mezcal maker.

Traditionally, mezcal makers did not isolate species. They harvested whatever maguey was ripest and nearest to the palenque. This approach resulted in field blends. As Americans developed a taste for mezcal, they placed a focus on varietal mezcals, which is predominantly how wine is understood. Unfortunately, this has placed undue strain on wild varieties that have become popular among Americans and Europeans. Field blends might be considered a more traditional approach to mezcal, as well as a more sustainable one.

FIVE MEN PREPARING A ROAST, SANTA CATARINA MINAS.

Espadín (*Agave angustifolia* Haw.) is the most common variety found in Oaxaca and is predominantly farmed. It matures in six to eight years and can grow to have two-hundred-pound piñas. It has long, narrow spiky leaves and produces a range of flavors, from fruity and spicy to herbaceous and earthy.

Tobalá (*A. potatorum*) is known as the king of magueys. Indigenous people believe it was the first maguey. Tobalá likes rocky, high-altitude soil and only grows in the shade of oak trees, like truffles. It takes ten to fifteen years to ripen and about eight times as many piñas to equal the weight of one espadín. It has broad, flat, spiny leaves and roots that emit an enzyme capable of breaking down granite so that the plant can reach deep down into the earth to find water. Tobalá produces a complex mezcal marked by herbaceousness and intense minerality.

Madrecuixe (*A. karwinskii*) matures in ten to fifteen years. The karwinskii species includes several varieties of agave that grow long and cylindrical. Madrecuixe looks like a thick baseball bat. Its short spiky leaves grow from the ground up. It produces a green-tasting mezcal, full of herbs, with dusty and vegetal flavors.

Tobasiche (*A. karwinskii*) is harvested after ten to fifteen years. Unlike madrecuixe, it sheds its lower leaves as it grows, leaving a bare, dry bat of a piña with leaves sprouting from the top like palm fronds. It produces herbaceous, vegetal, dusty mezcal.

Barril (*A. karwinskii*) ripens in fifteen to twenty years. It's the biggest and fattest of the karwinskii agaves, producing a dry and earthy mezcal with plenty of umami.

Arroqueño (*A. americana* var. *oaxacensis*) takes up to twenty years to reach maturity. It's a large, silver-hued variety with long, spiny leaves that produces a rich, sweet, vegetal mezcal, often showing a note of chocolate.

Tepextate (*A. marmorata*) is a gargantuan variety that grows almost perpendicular to the vertical cliffs. It can take thirty years or more to reach maturity. It has broad, twisted leaves and produces a candied, ethereal mezcal.

Papalome (*A. cupreata* × *A. potatorum*) looks like oversize tobalá, a rosette-style plant with broad, flat leaves. It takes ten to twelve years to ripen and produces an earthy, meaty mezcal with exceptional complexity.

CHAPTER 4

FATHERS AND SONS

Cruising along the Pan-American Highway one day in 1990, sun blazing, I stopped and treated myself to lunch, right at the crossroads to Tlacolula de Matamoros. The village plays host to a big Sunday market where Oaxacans come to shop for everything from fresh food to handmade ceramics and textiles. Market days always feel celebratory. But on the day I stopped for lunch, the streets were quiet. After my meal of memelitas and squash blossom empanadas con queso at a small restaurant, I was served a complimentary mezcal. I was wary because a lot of the mezcal I come across in places like this is terrible. This was not. I ended up asking the waiter to pour me a second taste. It was *puro chingón*. Fucking fantastic. Fruity and creamy with a spice tickle on the nose. I asked where it was made: San Luis del Río. Five years later, when I was starting Del Maguey, I remembered that mezcal.

Some people say I taste in colors. It's not necessarily that I perceive a flavor as yellow or green, although sometimes I do. It's the way my brain processes and stores sensory information. It allows me to absorb a mezcal the way I might a painting or a photograph. I can remember how it sat in the mouth. How it made me feel. When the memory of the mezcal I had in Tlacolula wormed itself out from the back of my mind, its aromas and flavors were as readily available to me as the day I'd first had it. I was determined to track it down so I could taste it again.

I pinpointed San Luis del Río on a map, some sixty miles from Teotitlán del Valle, up in the mountains. It was time for an adventure. Pancho went everywhere with me in those days. For this trip, I took almost his entire family with me. His wife, mother, and two daughters all piled into my 1978 white Coupe DeVille. This beauty of a car was tricked out with orange marker lights on the roof, an all-new undercarriage suspension, and truck tires to make it drive like a 4x4. It came in handy once we left the paved highway. I called it The Roadillac.

The trip was a special occasion for Pancho and his family. His mother, Asunción, looked regal in her traditional Zapotec dress, her long hair woven with ribbons into a thick braid that sat coiled on top of her head like a crown. She was so genteel, but she could make me laugh until it hurt. She giggled at every little thing she found funny or absurd, and her giggling was infectious. I'd known Pancho's two girls since they were babies, crawling around on the dirt floor at their grandmother's house. No one told me this would be their first time in a car.

With a map and Pancho navigating, we left Teotitlán del Valle early on a Saturday morning. We drove past the turnoff to Mitla, Oaxaca's most important archaeological site after Monte Alban, and on through Santiago Matatlán, which bills itself as the "world capital of mezcal" thanks to a cluster of commercial palenques along the main road. Heading south on the Pan-American Highway, we passed Nueve Puntas and the

WORKING BY SOLAR-POWERED LIGHT IN SAN LUIS DEL RÍO.

UNLOADING LARGE ESPADÍN IN SAN LUIS DEL RÍO.
(NOTE THE TRUNK WOOD USED FOR HEATING THE *HORNO*.)

turnoffs for Chichicapa, Totolapan, and Zoquitlán. The road wound and twisted back on itself as the altitude rose. The girls got queasy. They kept it together as long as they could, but eventually begged me to stop so they could get out and throw up.

After a couple hours, we came to the unmarked exit for San Luis del Río and hung a left onto a dirt track carved roughly into the side of the mountain. To our left, spiky maguey plants loomed overhead on the steep hills amid the brush and cacti. To our right gaped a vast abyss, crowned by the Sierra Madre in the distance. Inside the car, all was quiet. The only sounds were the engine growling, the dirt road scraping up against the tires. After nearly an hour, we felt pavement under the tires again. The Roadillac descended into San Luis like a spaceship. It was the only vehicle in town. Up on the hillside sat simple cement and adobe homes. Below us, way down the hill at the bottom of the village, was the Rio Hormiga Colorada: Red Ant River. We drove a few blocks into town, past the cemetery and school. Finally, we came to the church. Here was the heart of the village, where the local government—the *municipio*—was based. We stopped the car a respectful distance away, and Pancho and I hung back as the women and children went to pay their respects at the church's altar.

As we approached the municipio, about a dozen men sat on a bench out front, eyeing us. Pancho spoke to them in Zapotec, explaining that we were from Teotitlán del Valle and were looking to buy mezcal to export to the United States. He went on to recount how I'd tasted their mezcal years ago and never forgot it, and asked if any among them had a palenque or any mezcal to sell us. We were met with stony silence. The village sits at 8,000 feet above sea level. The air, thin as it is up there, shifted. It turned out that the people of San Luis believed they were originally from Teotitlán. Drought was said to have driven out their ancestors who migrated to the river valley generations ago and settled it before spreading into the mountains. But this connection did not stir them. Neither did the long journey we had made with our strange car or the fact that a gringo wanted to buy their mezcal. We were not welcome, that much was clear.

After a five-minute standoff, the village elders just staring us down, we thanked them and started to back away. We fetched the women and children, gave a perfunctory salute to the church altar, jumped in the car, and turned back the way we came. As we were leaving, a man began to chase after us. He was a bear of a man, surprisingly nimble and quick for his size. "Hey, hey!" he called as he caught up to us. "I make mezcal!" This was Paciano Cruz Nolasco.

Paciano has a broad face, angular nose, and sloe-eyed gaze. His most distinctive feature by far are his hands. They are the outsize, thick mitts of a farmer. Rough palms as big as dinner plates, dirty nails, deep scars on every other finger. He lost vision in an eye after getting poked by a maguey thorn some years ago. He can still perceive light and dark out of the milky blue left orb, but has to rely on the right one, dark brown, to see. Like me, he wears the same outfit every day. (Those who know me know I like to wear a pair of blue jeans and a loose-fitting white cotton shirt, traditional Oaxacan peasant garb. I have about two dozen of these shirts, which I buy from a shop in Oaxaca City. I prefer to wash them myself. I'm precise in my laundry routine and my shirts come out bright white, like new, each time, no matter how filthy they get.) Paciano's uniform is a comfortable pair of beige chino pants and a thin pale green nylon shirt. He will never admit to where he buys his shirts.

Another thing Paciano and I have in common is a belief in a god-given gift. A *don*. He says he was *nació con estrella*, born with a star. His gift is knowing maguey, being able to bring it to life, then extract its spirit. Mine is being able to feel out the brightest stars to lead me to the best mezcal. Paciano is younger than me by about a decade, but he doesn't speak to me with the deference many Oaxacans reserve for their elders—or employers, for that matter. It's refreshing. He feels more like a partner than our other producers. A brother, even. When either of us tastes a great mezcal we'll say, "*Puro chingón*!" It's a vulgar expression, but irreverence keeps me pure. The life of a Zapotec farmer out in the mountains is a hard one. The sun and hard labor take their toll on the body, the skin, the bones. Paciano's body is aging, but his spirit is as irreverent as ever. He's still two guys wide and a total badass. A locomotive.

A son of San Luis, Paciano left his village at age eleven for Mexico City. There, he sold water to make a living. He'd tried making mezcal like his grandparents had, but there wasn't much of a market for it at the time. He traveled back and forth between Oaxaca and Mexico City, making mezcal when he could. Paciano lived at the top of the hill in San Luis, the highest house in the village. He, his wife, and their three children all slept in a one-room stucco house, the kids snuggled up to their parents like puppies. A separate building housed a wood fire for cooking. Dirt floors, meager belongings, no bathroom or running water. Like everyone else in town, they had no car. Paciano used a horse to transport maguey and other cargo. He'd achieved a respectable status in the village after building the road into town. He'd spent a year living out in the brush with little more than a pickax and shovel, cutting the rugged path out of the mountain face that we drove in on. Until then, villagers who needed to travel—to go to a hospital in Oaxaca or visit a market in Tlacolula—would load up a burro and lead it down to the river, then follow the riverbank to the highway to catch a bus. The trip to the highway took a day.

By 1995, Paciano had been struggling financially for some time. That's when the Roadillac pulled into town. After that first visit, I promised Paciano I'd come back to taste his mezcal once he finished his next batch. Back then, communicating with palenqueros was a major challenge. I had a Motorola the size of a brick that couldn't pick up a signal in any of the villages. Most villages had one shared phone and calls had to be arranged ahead of time. To set up the meeting with Paciano, I called the village's only phone, located in a ramshackle phone booth in a small tienda. The person who answered told me to call back the next day at a set time and Paciano would be there. When Paciano and I spoke, he invited me to meet him at his home. From there, we would make our way down to the palenque he rented by the river.

The road from the top of the village to the river twists and turns sharply at acute angles. The palenque was simple. Under the shade of a huge tree sat a big stone mill, three wooden fermentation tanks, and a small copper pot still. A few yards away was a mound of earth covering halved maguey hearts that had been roasting for several days over hot stones. A horse stood nearby, hitched up to a tree, its skin twitching as flies came to rest on it. Its job was to pull the one-ton stone around the floor of the *molino* (mill) to crush the roasted maguey. Out here, under the trees, with the river gurgling nearby, I tasted Paciano's mezcal. The flavors I remembered from five years previous in that small restaurant in Tlacolula came rushing back to me, the colors

PACIANO CRUZ NOLASCO WITH GRANDCHILDREN MARCOS AND VIDA, SAN LUIS DEL RÍO. ASUNCIONA MENDEZ, PACIANO'S WIFE, IN HER WOOD-FIRE ADOBE KITCHEN.

72

just as vibrant. It turned out that Paciano had been taking his mezcal to Tlacolula to sell in the market, traveling by bus and burro, for years. His mezcal spoke to me like a ghost before I even met him. I asked if I could buy three hundred liters from him on the spot and, without leaving a deposit, promised to return a month later to collect it.

My next trip to San Luis del Río was even more arduous than the first. I'd borrowed a VW van to transport six fifty-six-liter used Pabst and Pearl beer barrels to store the mezcal. The van was a clunker. It was a hundred-degree day and the van kept breaking down, the carburetor shot. Pancho and I left Teotitlán at five o'clock in the morning, crawled along the highway going half our usual speed, and pulled into San Luis by late morning. When we got there, we filled the barrels with mezcal and stashed them in the back of the van along with Paciano. We drove the fifty-odd miles to Tlacolula so he could go to the bank to cash his very first check. Our car trouble didn't let up. We made it to the bank with just fifteen minutes to spare before it closed. Paciano was brimming with pride.

After that, I kept going back to San Luis to buy mezcal and hang out with Paciano. Each time I visited, his wife would cook us a delicious meal of tamales wrapped in banana leaf or mole amarillo—always with huge, leathery wild corn tlayudas—and we would talk over copitas of mezcal. Over time, we forged a friendship. On one trip, I brought a photographer friend of mine from Taos named Paul O'Connor. My original idea had been to have a different artist friend do the label for each village's mezcal. Paul's photos always managed to capture a truth in their subjects. The ones he took in San Luis were so captivating that we ended up making the first labels and a poster from them. They show a young boy, Paciano's ten-year-old son, Marcos, in the middle of the river with a burro hauling maguey. When he first saw the camera, Marcos began bounding up and

MARCOS CRUZ MENDEZ, SAN LUIS DEL RÍO, 1995.

down, begging his dad to be in the photo. But in the image, he's gazing intently into the camera's lens. In another shot, a horse is pulling the molino as it grinds maguey, while a ghostly wisp of a figure in a white dress chases after the animal. It's one of Paciano's daughters, either Ema or Marilu. Neither of us can remember which one.

Paciano used the proceeds from his early Del Maguey sales to fix up his home. He laid down cement floors so his family wouldn't have to sleep on the dirt floor, and built additional rooms. He installed a bathroom with running water to replace the outhouse. He also bought a three-ton, fire-engine-red Ford truck. Paciano taught himself to drive and, once he was mobile, went into business for himself transporting maguey for other farmers. He was also able to ferry a great deal more mezcal into Tlacolula to sell at the weekly market than before when he was traveling by burro.

Despite the fact that I was his biggest customer, Paciano liked to tease me for buying such tiny quantities. He was ambitious. So, when I could, I tried to hook him up with odd jobs. It didn't always work out. A guy I knew from back home asked if I could find someone to plant agave for him in Mazatlán. I told Paciano he could get a nice chunk of cash for running the plants up the coast and planting them. It was agreed he would be reimbursed the cost of gas and served a hot meal upon arrival— it's customary to feed laborers, especially for jobs in remote areas. Paciano hired a crew of five men and made it to Mazatlán in a day and a half. When they arrived, the buyer wasn't there. And the meal they were promised turned out to be a pitiful portion of scrambled eggs and one measly tortilla each. These were men accustomed to putting away half a dozen enormous tlayudas for breakfast each morning. Such hearty meals were necessary to provide the energy needed to work. Paciano never forgot how badly he and his men were treated and he never lets me forget. To this day, he breaks out this story when we're together. I learned to better screen people who wanted access to Paciano and my other producers. Especially now that mezcal has become popular and entrepreneurs travel to Oaxaca in search of business opportunities, I'm aware that Paciano and the others must be protected.

In 2005, the regulations governing mezcal production went into effect, which would change the lives of many mezcal-making families. My life changed, too: I'd been working free of bureaucracy for a decade. The new legal framework was poorly designed. It was based on tequila's regulations and didn't reflect the realities of making mezcal. For example, it tried to limit the types of maguey that could be used to a short list of recognizable varieties, but mezcal makers use whichever variety growing nearest the palenque that happens to be ripe. Technologies designed for mass production used in tequila were also permitted—namely, diffusers. These monster machines use hot water and sulfuric acid to process raw agave. They have nothing to do with traditional mezcal culture. In fact, the regulations did nothing to protect or promote traditional production practices. Like tequila, the rules were focused on the end product and tried to enforce prescribed levels of alcohol and acidity. Traditional mezcal comes off the still at high proofs—45 percent alcohol by volume or more—and the acidity is high. Adding water to bring the proof down or adjusting the pH, for many producers, is unthinkable.

By this time, Paciano's family had adopted me into their clan. We spent the Day of the Dead together, as well as *Semana Santa* (Easter), San Luis del Río's *fiesta anual*, the annual celebration of the village's patron saint. It became clear that Paciano was the most intrepid producer in the Del Maguey family. He would be the first to undergo the grueling new verification process. I decided we would go through it together and moved in with him for three weeks as we filled out the dense paperwork. Picking through it was like wading into dark, muddy waters. Certain sections contradicted others, and the legalese was unbearable. We struggled through the language, submitted the requisite maps and surveys, and did a complete production run for the regulatory verifiers. Each step of the way, information was entered into the distillery registry book as witnesses testified to its accuracy and the official verifier signed. Paciano was fearless.

It wasn't all work, those three weeks. Living with Paciano afforded me moments of pure joy. Each morning, his mother shared the good coffee I'd brought with me, the only one in the family who appreciated it as much as I did. Paciano no longer made mezcal at the little palenque he had long rented from a neighbor. The money he made from working with Del Maguey had allowed him to set up his own place downriver, a bigger facility he'd built from scratch. It was a clever operation in an idyllic setting. The maguey fibers left over after crushing, the hairlike bagazo, were dumped on the outskirts of the palenque, leading down to the river. Over time, they turned to compost and made new soil. Coconut palms, lime trees, chiles, oregano, and cilantro flourished. There was also *chico sapote*, a fruit that looks like a kiwi and tastes like the love child of a tangerine and a fig. It was paradise. Once the stills got going, we would scoop the hot water from the condensation tank into a five-gallon bucket and carry it over to a secluded spot under a coconut palm to bathe, the bagazo turning to earth beneath our feet.

There were days when the heat was so intense that we rose at two o'clock in the morning to get a jump on the day. We would weave our way down to the palenque to stoke the stills. These were the best hours to work, with midday temperatures soaring past 110°F. Once the sun was high, we'd abandon our posts and go fishing in the river. One morning, Paciano's wife packed us a big cooking pot, a dozen huge tlayudas, tomatoes, limes, onions, and chiles. I followed Paciano, a fishing net slung over his shoulder, down to the palenque. We got the stills going and, around midday, headed down to the river. Three young men who helped out at the palenque joined us. This is the time of day you find villagers bathing in the shallow waters. Everyone stripped down to their Jockey shorts, Paciano looking mammoth next to his skinny helpers. One of the guys donned a mask—no snorkel, just a mask—and dove in. He swam around scoping out what was going on under the water's surface. Suddenly, his arm popped straight up out of the water, the rest of him still submerged. His index finger pointed back down toward whatever was swimming beneath him. We knew where to cast our net. When we pulled it up, it was full of fish.

That day we caught mojarra, a small, flat fish that fries up beautifully. All of us were giggling like children. After filling a large bucket, we headed back to the palenque. One of the young men cleaned our catch while Paciano tossed tomatoes, chiles, and onions into the pot his wife had given us. In went the fish. Paciano fastened the pot to a stick and hung it in the still's firebox. We cut up the limes and, in fifteen minutes, lunch was ready. We feasted, tearing our tlayudas to sop up the fishy broth.

Paciano's son Marcos was still a boy when I started working with his father. Later, when he was old enough to make a living of his own, he did what so many sons and daughters of farmers in Mexico were forced to do. Marcos went to find work in the US. In rural families, even up until a decade or so ago, it was common for children to leave; there was little incentive to stay. They picked fruit, did construction, took hard jobs for unthinkable pay. They didn't always come home. The journey to get to the American border is filled with physical dangers—rattlesnakes, sunstroke. But it's the coyotes, brutish types who prey on the poor souls who undertake the northbound voyage, who pose the greatest risk. Young men have been kidnapped, women raped, children abused en route to what they envision to be a better life. Many never make it. Back home, parents worry, of course. But there is a second tragedy that unfolds when children leave home. It plays out in villages like San Luis del Río, where for generations families have cultivated maguey and made mezcal. The children absent, there is no one to take over the craft. A piece of the culture dies.

Paciano's heart grew heavier each month and year his son was away. One day, sitting out at the palenque while his daughters swept the molino in preparation for the grind, Paciano began to talk to me about Marcos. The two had not been on good terms when he left. Now that they were separated by more than two thousand miles, the gulf between them seemed insuperable. He knew Marcos was somewhere in Indiana, working as a roofer, but he had not heard much else. Marcos had sent no money home and little news. Paciano began to think he might never see his son again.

What's more, he was forced to imagine a future in which he was the last in his family to make mezcal. I decided I had to take him to the US for a visit.

I ended up taking five Zapotecs to Chicago for ten days. We toured the Midwest, hosting Oaxacan cooking classes and mezcal tastings. I had Paciano, Pancho, and Florencio Carlos Sarmiento, the old man from Santa Catarina Minas, with me. Pancho's wife, Ernestina—whose mole negro is, in my opinion, the best in Oaxaca—came along to give wood-fired cooking and mole demonstrations along with Miguel Jiménez Herrera, the chef at Los Danzantes, a popular restaurant in Oaxaca. They were in awe of everything they saw, from the skyscrapers to the buffet breakfasts. Everything was so *big*.

After a tasting event near Cincinnati, I could feel Paciano getting antsy. I had promised to take him to Clarksville, Indiana, to look for Marcos at his last known address. We got into my Jeep Grand Cherokee and started driving. We stopped at a motel in Kentucky and in the morning set out for Louisville, which is just across the Ohio River from Clarksville. When we got there, we found an enclave of apartments where all the Zapotecs lived. Marcos was there. Father and son cried like babies when they embraced. It was bittersweet: Marcos was forced to fess up about what he'd been doing all this time. He had bought a Bronco, crashed it when he was drunk, and saved none of the money he'd made. Paciano could not hide his dismay—if his son was just wasting time here, what was it all for? We found a traditional Mexican restaurant and all sat down to a meal together. Then it was time to take Marcos back to his apartment. Paciano was in agony.

We drove back up all the way through Kentucky and Indiana to Chicago. We still had Oaxacan cooking classes to teach and mezcal tastings to host. In Chicago, the chef Rick Bayless, who had come to visit me in Oaxaca and called the trip the most life-changing cultural experience of his life, invited us to his restaurant for a special lunch. The Zapotecs were having the time of their lives—all except Paciano. He was heartbroken. He couldn't bear the thought of returning to San Luis without Marcos. But he did.

After the trip, Paciano had a new appreciation for the people in America who bought his mezcal. "We have to make it more affordable," he told me. Out of pure love and benevolence, he wanted to share his spirit with as many people as possible. It was around this time that bartenders around the US were approaching me with a similar request: a mezcal made for mixing into cocktails, one the bars could afford. That's how we came up with the idea for Vida, which would be made in San Luis and bottled at a slightly lower proof. (Mezcal had always been expensive for bars and most could only afford to use small amounts of it in cocktails. In the US, taxes paid on spirits are based on alcohol content; the higher the proof, the higher the cost.) We discovered we could achieve a lower proof without adding any water to the spirit, a common practice among modern mezcal brands, but one I was loath to adopt: *mezcal con agua no es mezcal*. We figured out how to distill the mezcal to a proof of 84 by roasting the magueys longer, getting them nice and caramelized, then using more of the tail-end of the distillate, the colas, to adjust it. The product was priced lower than the other Single Village mezcal we sold. I named it after my granddaughter, Vida. Life.

In the villages, the distribution of land is strictly regulated. Only those with ancestral ties to a village are permitted to buy property there. Because Paciano had built the road into town, he was given the right to plant maguey wherever he wanted in San Luis. He was also elected village president, an important role, but the new responsibilities came at a bad time. He was busier than ever making Vida in addition to several other expressions, and was now charged with handling official village business, itself a full-time commitment. He needed help. Now more than ever, Paciano needed Marcos to come home. It would be another few years before he finally sent for him. He sat me down and shared a crazy idea he'd been entertaining for some time. He could not afford to leave San Luis and keep up production. Instead, he would send his daughters on a mission to go find their brother and bring him home. All he needed from me was six thousand dollars to pay a coyote to ferry them across the border.

Paciano and his wife were always taking in children from families in other villages even more remote than their own, places with no schools or doctors. Marilu, the youngest of the two daughters, took on the job of caring for the little ones. She was sweet and quite pretty, but had always seemed like a quiet, simple girl to me. Her older sister Ema was inquisitive and bright, taking the initiative of signing up for computer classes in Tlacolula. Neither hesitated to accept their father's challenge.

After several days on a bus that took them to *la frontera*, they found a coyote less corrupt than most. He took the girls across the treacherous Sonoran Desert. Cacti, rattlesnakes, and Border Patrol helicopters looming overhead posed the most immediate threats. But the elements were not to be underestimated. The sun was harsh and unrelenting. At nightfall, the cold came in fast, seeping into clothing, then bones. Ema was carrying some extra clothes and gifts she wanted to give to a friend on the other side of the border. She was told to leave them, to take nothing but water, but she ignored the advice. Soon she began to lag behind. It didn't take long for her to succumb to heat exhaustion. Marilu was determined to keep her sister going. She shared her water, slid her arm around Ema's waist and shouldered her weight as they

78 trudged through the desert, talking her sister through the most terrifying moments of the trek. The sisters made it to the US from Oaxaca in roughly two weeks. When they finally landed in Clarksville they searched out their brother. Marcos was shocked to see his sisters in Indiana. The reunion was an emotional one, but Marcos was adamant: he was staying. He had nothing to return to in Oaxaca. He knew his parents were disappointed in his behavior. He was probably a little disappointed in himself.

Ema and Marilu moved into the small community of Zapotecs where Marcos had settled and stayed on for a few months. In time, Marcos softened. His sisters convinced him he could make a decent living working with his father, making mezcal. He finally agreed to return with them to Oaxaca after hearing that Paciano's eye had been pierced by a maguey thorn, leaving him unable to drive. Before they even had a chance to make arrangements for their return, Ema met a young man from back home and got pregnant. Upon hearing the news, Paciano told her to stay in

America. Ema was to raise the child there until it had grown into a proper English-speaking American. Then, they could come home. Ema ended up marrying the young man and is still in Clarksville raising her family. Marilu and Marcos returned to San Luis together.

When Marcos came home, he was an angry young man. His fraught relationship with his parents had never been resolved and he felt sour over what he viewed as his failure to make a good life for himself in the US, a place he was now all but barred from returning to because of some legal trouble he'd gotten into while there. What's more, he was now back under his father's roof and authority. Paciano begged me to talk to his son. One day, I approached Marcos while

MEZCAL CON AGUA NO ES MEZCAL
(MEZCAL WITH WATER IS NOT MEZCAL).

he was in the fields. His father had immediately put him to work planting on a steep slope in a narrow gorge. Marcos was toiling away amid five thousand magueys when I broached the subject of the rift with his dad. "My mother hates me," he complained. "My father has never once said, 'I love you.'" He sounded like any angst-filled kid, so sure his parents didn't get him. "I understand what you're going through," I told him. "But you gotta take it easy with your dad." I made him a deal. If he could get along with his father enough for the two to work together, I would take him to Tequila and introduce him to the top producers there. I wanted to show him what he could be. Not rich like them, but respected. "And if you're really good," I said, "I'll take you to Europe." I kept my word and we took both trips. We got on an airplane, his first ever, and flew to Guadalajara, where we shared his mezcal with three of the greatest tequila makers in Jalisco. A year later, we flew to Amsterdam, Milan, and London, visiting bars and giving tastings. It was during this time that Marcos really began to see himself as a mezcal maker. Seeing so many new places and being introduced to so many new people boosted his confidence.

Marcos has grown into a fine young man. He makes sardonic jokes about never being allowed back into the US. "At least I can go back to Europe," he laughs. We have a special bond, he and I. When I put my arm around him in a fatherly way and ask how business is going, he refers to Del Maguey as "ours." And I'm just grinning. He now has a son of his own and a palenque he built with his own two hands, just across the river from his father's. Making Vida has allowed Marcos to hone his skills as a distiller. It's already obvious that he will be as great as his father. Their relationship is still tumultuous at times, but they appreciate the gift of being able to work together. For too long, the children of mezcal makers had to leave to find work elsewhere. Now, so many of them are home, working with their parents, and it warms my heart to be a part of that.

Paciano returned to the US with me a few years ago for the baptism of his granddaughter, Kennelly. I was named the godfather. *Padrino*. The whole Zapotec community in Clarksville turned out for the reception. Ema made tamales and we toasted the child with mezcal, just as the family would have done back home in San Luis. Paciano was beaming. But I know he longs for the day his entire family can be together under one roof again, back home in Oaxaca.

DEL MAGUEY SAN LUIS DEL RÍO

SINGLE VILLAGE MEZCAL

Three hours south of Oaxaca, on a two-lane, potholed highway en route to the Gulf of Tehuantepec, is the turnoff to San Luis del Río. It takes another two hours on a winding, rocky, dirt road to get to the village. San Luis is located in a narrow, hot valley. The steep slopes that cradle it are lined with fields of espadín. Here the mountains are scattered with cornfields, iguanas, blooming cacti, and bromeliads. The mezcal made here is bursting with playful aromas of fruit, spice, and smoke, brightened with a citrus note. It's creamy and lush in the mouth, where it unfolds like a flower, revealing its many layers and nuances before coming to a clean finish.

Production Notes

VILLAGE: San Luis Del Río

PALENQUEROS: Paciano Cruz Nolasco and Marcos Cruz Mendez

STATE: Oaxaca

REGION: Valles Centrales

MAGUEY: Espadín (*Agave angustifolia* Haw.)

AGE OF MAGUEY: 7–8 years

ELEVATION: 2,952 feet (900 meters)

ROAST DURATION: 3–8 days

TYPE OF WOOD: Quebrachi, huamúchil, pitayo, pochotle, tepeguaje, copal, pine, oak

MILLING: Wheel, Horse

SIZE OF TINAS: 1,400 L

FERMENTATION DURATION: 8–10 days

WATER SOURCE: Spring

STILL TYPE: Copper

STILL SIZE: 350 L

VOL ORDINARIO PER TINA: 200 L

ABV OF MEZCAL: 47%

VOL MEZCAL PRODUCED PER TINA: 100–120 L

DEL MAGUEY MADRECUIXE

VINO DE MEZCAL

Madrecuixe is a wild variety in the karwinskii family of magueys, tall and cylindrical, with leaves that grow from the ground up. This madrecuixe was bottled unblended. The flavor can only be described as green: banana leaf, green papaya, just-mown alfalfa, tarragon, and fresh-cut bamboo. These aromas give way to circus peanuts and sweet, ripe mango, pineapple, and chico sapote, the fruit that's like a fusion of tangerine and fig. Extremely rare, this wild mezcal is silky and elegant, with a long, dry, dusty finish.

Production Notes

VILLAGE: San Luis Del Río

PALENQUEROS: Paciano Cruz Nolasco and Marcos Cruz Mendez

STATE: Oaxaca

REGION: Valles Centrales

MAGUEY: Madrecuixe (*Agave karwinskii*)

AGE OF MAGUEY: 10–15 years

ELEVATION: 2,952 feet (900 meters)

ROAST DURATION: 3–8 days

TYPE OF WOOD: Quebrachi, huamúchil

MILLING: Wheel, Horse

SIZE OF TINAS: 1,400 L

FERMENTATION DURATION: 6–8 days

WATER SOURCE: Spring

STILL TYPE: Copper

STILL SIZE: 350 L

VOL ORDINARIO PER TINA: 200 L

ABV OF MEZCAL: 47%

VOL MEZCAL PRODUCED PER TINA: 100–120 L

DEL MAGUEY VIDA

SINGLE VILLAGE MEZCAL

Vida was developed with bartenders in mind. It's priced more affordably than our other Single Village expressions and has a lower alcohol content, making it ideal for mixing into cocktails. Bursting with fruity aromatics, it shows notes of honey, vanilla, and plenty of roasted agave character. On the palate, ginger, cinnamon, and burnt sandalwood come through, with hints of banana and tangerine lingering on the soft finish.

Production Notes

VILLAGE: San Luis Del Río

PALENQUEROS: Paciano Cruz Nolasco and Marcos Cruz Mendez

STATE: Oaxaca

REGION: Valles Centrales

MAGUEY: Espadín (*Agave angustifolia* Haw.)

AGE OF MAGUEY: 7–8 years

ELEVATION: 2,952 feet (900 meters)

ROAST DURATION: 3–8 days

TYPE OF WOOD: Quebrachi, huamúchil, pitayo, pochotle, tepeguaje, copal, pine, oak

MILLING: Wheel, Horse

SIZE OF TINAS: 1,400 L

FERMENTATION DURATION: 8–10 days

WATER SOURCE: Spring

STILL TYPE: Copper

STILL SIZE: 350 L

VOL ORDINARIO PER TINA: 200 L

ABV OF MEZCAL: 42%

VOL MEZCAL PRODUCED PER TINA: 120–150 L

DEL MAGUEY AZUL

VINO DE MEZCAL

Agave azul or blue agave, the species used in tequila production, is the genetic descendent of espadín, the most common species found in Oaxaca. During the agave shortage in tequila country in the early 2000s, trucks from Jalisco could be spotted roaming the Oaxacan countryside in search of espadín. When the men from Jalisco tried to purchase maguey from Paciano, he asked them to make a trade. They had brought baby blue agave with them, which they intended to plant in Oaxaca in case of a future shortage in Jalisco. Paciano planted some of it himself. Seven years later, the azul was mature. That first nine-hundred-bottle batch gave us the rare opportunity to fuse the flavors of Jalisco and Oaxaca. The result is a pit-roasted, naturally fermented, twice-distilled, and unblended mezcal that delivers bright citrus aromas and hints of banana chip. On the palate, it has a distinctly creamy mouthfeel, tasting of sweet herbs, wet stone, and a touch of white peppercorn on the finish.

Production Notes

VILLAGE: San Luis Del Río

PALENQUEROS: Paciano Cruz Nolasco and Marcos Cruz Mendez

STATE: Oaxaca

REGION: Valles Centrales

MAGUEY: Azul (*Agave tequilana*)

AGE OF MAGUEY: 7–8 years

ELEVATION: 2,952 feet (900 meters)

ROAST DURATION: 3–8 days

TYPE OF WOOD: Quebrachi, huamúchil, pitayo, pochotle, tepeguaje, copal, pine, oak

MILLING: Wheel, horse

SIZE OF TINAS: 1,400 L

FERMENTATION DURATION: 6–8 days

WATER SOURCE: Spring

STILL TYPE: Copper

STILL SIZE: 350 L

VOL ORDINARIO PER TINA: 200 L

ABV OF MEZCAL: 47%

VOL MEZCAL PRODUCED PER TINA: 70–90 L

DEL MAGUEY CREMA DE MEZCAL

SINGLE VILLAGE MEZCAL

Crema de Mezcal is a traditional sweet and creamy liqueur made by adding a dose of *miel de maguey* (the unfermented syrup pressed from roasted agave) to Del Maguey San Luis del Río Single Village Mezcal. The result is lush and honeyed, with a nose full of roasted maguey, vanilla, pear, pineapple, almond butter, coffee, and a hint of smoke on the finish.

Production Notes

VILLAGE: San Luis Del Río

PALENQUEROS: Paciano Cruz Nolasco and Marcos Cruz Mendez

STATE: Oaxaca

REGION: Valles Centrales

MAGUEY: Espadín (*Agave angustifolia* Haw.)

AGE OF MAGUEY: 6–8 years

ELEVATION: 2,952 feet (900 meters)

ROAST DURATION: 3–8 days

TYPE OF WOOD: Quebrachi, huamúchil, pitayo, pochotle, tepeguaje, copal, pine, oak

MILLING: Wheel, Horse

SIZE OF TINAS: 1,400 L

FERMENTATION DURATION: 8–10 days

WATER SOURCE: Spring

STILL TYPE: Copper

STILL SIZE: 350 L

VOL ORDINARIO PER TINA: 200 L

ABV OF MEZCAL: 40%

VOL MEZCAL PRODUCED PER TINA: 100–120 L

CHAPTER 5

CLAY POTS

Some four hundred years ago, a statuette of the Virgin Mary was brought to Oaxaca. The wooden figurine, standing maybe a foot tall, belonged to a Catholic friar. He made a gift of it to his servant, a Chatino Indian from the village of Amialtepec, who gave the statue a place on his family altar. His neighbors took to visiting the Virgin, and came to believe she granted miracles. As her fame grew, it was decided that she should be relocated to the church in the village. There she was displayed among the other Catholic saints, but the locals felt a special affinity toward her. One winter day, as the villagers burned their fields to prepare them for sowing in the spring, they lost control of the fire. It swept through the pasture and into the village, burning it to the ground. The church was consumed along with everything in it, save for the statuette of the Holy Virgin. Even her clothes were intact. A miracle. When she was found, the villagers saw that the skin on her face had been changed by the flames. Her complexion was darkened, making her look more like the natives, which served to inspire in them even greater reverence. They believed it was a sign that the statuette was the incarnation of Tonantzin, the earth mother goddess.

Different versions of this legend circulate. It's said that after the fire, the Holy Virgin was moved to a church in nearby Juquila. Since then, the Dark Virgin's fame spread far and wide. To this day, Oaxacans make the pilgrimage to visit the Virgin of Juquila at least once in their lives to ask her to grant them a miracle. And just about every Oaxacan family I know has her image displayed in their altar room.

When I'm in Oaxaca, the first thing I do upon entering a family's home is to pay my respects at their altar. I stand before it, say a silent prayer, cross myself (even though I'm not Catholic, I enjoy this ritual), or just close my eyes and think of nothing for a moment. The altar is usually located in a prominent spot, in a sitting room or dining room. It might include photographs that are meaningful to the family, flowers, candles. If my host offers me some mezcal, one of us will assume the role of *juez*: judge. The juez pours the mezcal, spilling a few drops on the ground to honor our ancestors. Always in the sign of the cross. The four directions. When we raise our copitas, we look into each other's eyes with meaning and intent, and say, *Stigibeu!* It means, "To your health, to the health of your family, and to the health of Mother Earth." Then we say, *bakeen*: roughly, "Drink, serve yourself." With a barely perceptible nod, we raise a hand in a subtle gesture, palm facing in, fingers stretched, that says, "I honor you." This common Zapotec signal is a show of respect.

I've adopted the custom as my own. Whether I'm in a village or tasting with a sommelier in a Michelin-starred restaurant, I spill a little mezcal on the ground for our ancestors. I say, *Stigibeu!* and honor the person I'm drinking with. To the astonishment of friends around the world, I've poured mezcal on the finest rugs and most

ANASTASIO CRUZ ANTONIO,
BUENA VISTA LAS MILPAS.

highly polished floors. "Cálmate," I tell them. "The alcohol of a truly good mezcal evaporates. It leaves no trace."

There are several permutations to the ritual I've described: in Chichicapa, for example, it's pronounced "*stigi-bua-a-loo*." In Matatlán, it's "*dixibe*." In Santa Catarina Minas, it's not said at all. Minas is the one village I work with where the indigenous language was abandoned long ago. The Minero people are proud of their Spanish, which is genteel and old-fashioned. When they toast, they say, "*Salúd*!"

I first heard about Santa Catarina Minas from Pancho's father, Cosme, the old weaver who asked me to take his son across the border with me. When I started searching for mezcal, Pancho and his father often accompanied me. Cosme didn't drink much, but he had a great palate and considered himself something of a mezcal aficionado. The three of us ventured out together to find Minas, a village known to make a special mezcal. We rolled into town and found our way to a palenque. Everyone there was fall-down drunk, and we knew immediately that it was no place we wanted to be. We asked if there were any other mezcal makers in town and were pointed down a washboard road. We pulled up outside the home of Florencio Carlos Sarmiento, who lived there with his wife, two sons, and two daughters. It was a sprawling rancho with dairy cows, pigs, turkeys, and chickens running around the courtyard. Florencio—Don Lencho, as we came to know him—was in his sixties, his children grown. He greeted us warily, but as soon as we revealed we were in the market for mezcal, I could see the wheels in his head turning.

"If you want mezcal, I've got the best," he said. "But it's gonna cost you."

What he poured us was incredible—at once rich and robust, but also floral and honeyed. And it had a texture like velvet on the tongue. Don Lencho showed us his palenque, and I began to grasp what made his mezcal so special. The still he used was made of clay instead of copper. It sat on a mud stove heated with firewood. No bigger than a kitchen cauldron, it was equipped with a hollow carrizo reed from which dripped the fresh mezcal. He called the contraption *olla de barro*: mud pot. It was beautiful. But the old man put me on edge. He was a curmudgeon through and through. With his sun-leathered face and crinkly eyes, he shifted easily from surly to sly to sweet. He would snap at us one minute, then let a cheeky smirk creep across his face as he tried to pull the wool over our eyes the next. I didn't think I could work with him. He wanted to charge me twenty times more than any of the other producers I'd met! I thanked him for his time and left not knowing if I'd ever see him again. But the mezcal stayed with me. I couldn't stop thinking about how it tasted and felt in the mouth, and the archaic way it was made.

It took me a year to return to Minas. In the end, it was inevitable. The mezcal was just too good. By this time, I was beginning to understand how the spirit could vary so much from village to village, producer to producer. It would be years before I learned about the French wine concept of terroir—how the soil, climate, and hand of the maker are imprinted on a wine. But before anyone explained it to me, I began to perceive how this worked with mezcal. The soil and climate of a place influence how the maguey grows there, the flavors it produces. But it's the rich microbial life of the palenque that gives a mezcal much of its identity. Native yeasts, bacteria, and other airborne microbes live in the walls of the palenque, in the thatch of the roof, and on the maguey plants themselves out in the fields. Antibacterial-obsessed Americans might see palenques as unsanitary, but making mezcal in a sterile environment is impossible. It's the population of microorganisms that ushers along fermentation that is responsible for the transformation of juice into alcohol. The microorganisms are the conduit. If you were to take a scientific sample, these microorganisms change every three hundred feet of altitude. It's no wonder one palenquero's mezcal tastes completely different from his neighbor's, even if they're both using the same variety of maguey and virtually the same production methods.

Fermentation begins when the maguey hearts are resting, perhaps in the shade of a tree, for a week or so after the roast is unearthed. The piñas get transferred to the molino, which itself harbors native yeasts and microbes in its crevices. More yeasts live within the walls of the tinas, the three-hundred-gallon wooden fermentation vats. The various yeasts and bacteria present in the palenque work together to convert the sugars in the maguey mash to alcohol. The mysterious chemical reactions involved are what release flavor compounds like esters and phenols. Each yeast and bacteria strain can produce different flavor compounds. In the world of wine, the term "microbial terroir" has emerged. In Oaxaca there is a saying, "*Sabor que nace.*" Flavor that is born.

After a couple days, a dose of water from a nearby source is added to the fermenting maguey mash, galvanizing all those yeasts. The water source must be pristine. There are producers in Oaxaca who use treated municipal water, but the ones I work with—and those typically considered the best and most authentic—use only natural spring water, well, or river water. It imparts minerality to the mezcal. In time, the contents of the tina start to bubble and foam. Heat rises off it. If you press your ear against the wall of the tank and hold very still, you can hear the fermentation crackling and gurgling inside.

CLAY POT STILL IN EL BIGOTE'S *PALENQUE*,
SAN PEDRO TEOZACOALCO.

In Minas, as I've said, clay pots are used instead of copper for distillation. Something about the organic nature of clay, its porousness, causes the mezcal to come out creamy and lush. The use of clay pots to make mezcal dates back centuries and, for some reason, the mezcal makers of Minas never phased them out. Santa Catarina Minas is like a living museum. Archaeologists and other researchers actively seek out places like this to help with the ongoing research into mezcal's history. A growing number of scientists now believe mezcal has been made for more than two millennia—the world's first spirit.

At Don Lencho's palenque, I watched the fermented juice and maguey fibers get fed into the still, a one hundred–liter pot. It was embedded in a wood-burning fireplace, a handmade dome built from adobe bricks, mud, and bagazo. Above it was a smaller clay pot with the bottom removed, the condensation chamber, topped by a copper bowl filled with water. As the mixture in the still reached its boiling point, vapors from it rose and collected at the base of the bowl. A carrizo reed caught the droplets as they collected and fell. The spirit slipped down the length of the carrizo and trickled out the end, one drop at a time. Florencio watched the process closely, clocking the puntas (heads) and colas (tails). The old man knew precisely when to cut them from the heart to achieve the ideal balance of flavors and alcohol. In modern distilleries in the US and Europe, machines are calibrated to measure when these cuts should be made. In Minas, there are no machines. Just Florencio. He sniffs the air and instinctively knows when the time is right.

We paid Don Lencho the price at which he valued his elixir, just as we do with all our makers. The spirit is their art, after all, and they are the only ones who can decide its worth. The mezcal from Minas—Minero—was one of Del Maguey's original four Single Village mezcals. Since then, it has become legendary among mezcal lovers around the world for its rich complexity and that seductive texture clay-pot distillation gives. But working with the old man has never been easy. As his children can attest, living with him was not easy, either.

One year, I took my brother and his wife to visit Florencio. My sister-in-law is from Panama, so she was able to converse easily with the women in the house. We sat in the courtyard as Florencio's wife shelled peas and chatted casually with my sister-in-law. The Spanish they spoke was sped up, not as languid as when either of them spoke to me. Still, I gleaned that the old woman had a terrible tear duct infection, a painful ailment but one easily remedied with surgery. Florencio was too cheap to pay for the operation, she complained. It came as no surprise when, months later, the old woman left her husband and moved to another rancho outside the village. She was soon followed by her son, Florencio Jr., an agronomist. The other son, Luis, had gone to work in the city as a bureaucrat. The two daughters were left to care for their father. Florencio, crotchety as he was, forbade his adult daughters from marrying. They were to take their mother's place milking cows, making cheese, feeding pigs, raising turkeys, growing herbs, cooking meals on the wood fire, going to the market, and performing all the other tasks required to run the rancho.

Some time later, I was contacted by an Israeli film crew. They wanted to shoot a documentary about mezcal. I agreed to take them to Santa Catarina Minas. The camera rolled from dawn to dusk, filming the daily routine at the palenque. Accompanying the crew as a translator and facilitator was a redhead from Mexico City. The palenque workers insisted she was a *bruja*: a witch. I never quite understood why, but they claimed she put the evil eye on a maguey roast. The roast went cold, the slow-burning heat of it suddenly extinguished—an unlikely occurrence. Days later, Don Lencho's spleen burst. The thing is, aged and sour as he was, he was a perfectly healthy old fucker. It was the bruja's curse that did it, I'm sure. Florencio's son, Luis, was summoned from Oaxaca City. He decided to take his father to Mexico City to see a specialist, the village doctor treating the old man in tow. There Florencio lay in his hospital bed, tubes in both arms, lungs failing, heart failing, his ashen face obscured by an oxygen mask. At one point, he looked up at his son, mustered whatever strength he had to pull the tubes from his arms, and sat up.

"If I'm going to die, I want to die in my own bed," he said.

Luis took his father back to Minas and I met them there. The scene was anachronistic. The old man's abdomen cut open, the cavity being drained of a foul-smelling fluid—a superannuated procedure. Only one daughter was allowed in the room. I wasn't permitted to see him. Suddenly, as if things couldn't get any worse for him, poor Florencio began to hiccup. His hiccups lasted a full two weeks. In that time, he lost half his body weight. His skin grayed. His eyes paled. He was shrinking. He was dying. Luis, for his part, knew he couldn't return to the city. Instead, he took his father's place in the palenque and finished the batch of mezcal Don Lencho had been making before taking ill. The batch came out perfect.

Florencio, who could barely eat or drink, called for his son. "Take me to see the Virgin of Juquila," he ordered. From Minas, the pilgrimage to Juquila takes one week on foot. Florencio had made the trip many times before and knew every inch of the path. In the past, he'd walked it alone. This time, he was ferried in a rented van with a driver and passed under the veil of the Virgin of Juquila in a wheelchair. He came out the other side with a twinkle in his eye. By the time he got home, his cheeks were rosy. Within weeks, he was back to his old gruff self. A miracle.

THE HISTORY OF MEZCAL

The long-held belief among scholars has been that the Spanish brought distillation to Mexico. In recent years, that theory has been challenged. Archeological digs in Tlaxcala, a small state east of Mexico City, as well as near the Colima volcano, which sits on the border between Jalisco and Michoacán, uncovered artifacts that suggest distillation predates the Spanish. Clay pots dating to 1500–1000 BCE were found that might have been used as primitive stills. Ancestral ovens dating to 400 BCE were discovered that, at first, were thought to be pottery kilns until they were compared to *hornos* in Oaxaca and found to contain traces of maguey. The findings have led a number of Mexican researchers to conclude that pre-Hispanic distillation surely took place.

The archaeological digs that turned up these artifacts were not aimed at discovering the origins of mezcal but conducted in the interest of learning about life in ancient times. The findings offered insights into early tribal cultures in Mexico, including the ritual uses of mezcal. The spirit was taken to mark baptisms and weddings, toddlers were given small drops for nourishment, and it was taken for *el cambio de vara*: the handing over of power among indigenous authorities.

Distillation likely spread around the country gradually, from pueblo to pueblo. Oaxaca became a hub of mezcal production, thanks to its abundance and diversity of agave. Still today, palenqueros tend to inherit the craft from their parents or other family members. In the remote mountain regions where mezcal is made, a village might have one producer or dozens, many of whom might be related.

Mezcal makers typically take their spirit to nearby markets or sell it directly to their neighbors, especially around each village's annual saint's day, usually celebrated with a days-long fiesta. As domestic and international demand for mezcal has risen in recent years, many producers now sell their mezcal to brands. Because most mezcal makers are not equipped—either financially or logistically—to distribute their product, being contracted by a domestic or international company is the only way to export their product. According to the Mezcal Regulatory Council, mezcal sales shot up to more than $164 million in 2016, up 42 percent from the previous year. Exports almost tripled between 2011 and 2016. And yet, mezcal only represented 0.4 percent of global spirits' market share in 2016.

Before they left for Juquila, I asked Luis who I should pay for the batch of mezcal he'd just finished. I knew he had medical bills and travel expenses piling up, and the old man was in no state to discuss business. Luis told me I could make the check out to him. As soon as his father was healthy enough, he threw his son out of the house. "How dare you take my money for the mezcal!" the old man said. Completely unreasonable, ungrateful. We took to calling Florencio "El Gato," because we figured he must have nine lives to have come so close to death and still be going strong. But he's like a cat in other ways, too. He might curl into your lap and start purring one minute only to swipe at you the next.

These days, Don Lencho is just about blind and hobbles around with the help of two canes, his hands shaking ever so slightly. His ankles are swollen, his fingers gnarled, his breathing labored. He moves slowly, his joints sore and his bones fragile. He's as cantankerous as ever. I've brought friends to visit and had him bark his disapproval at them only to turn around and shamelessly pinch the ass of one of the women in the group, a wicked smile in his eyes. He still makes mezcal with the help of nephews who do the heavy lifting. He can look at a pile of maguey and know precisely what it's worth, can sniff the air in the palenque and know when the mezcal is ready. And he still takes pleasure in playing with new maguey varieties. Recently, he was working on a batch of cerrudo that he'd purchased, a wild variety related to arroqueño that he believes to be the supreme maguey. But his body aches. He's running out of lives.

After everything they've been through together, Florencio doesn't speak to either of his sons. Yet, Luis and Florencio Jr. both learned to make mezcal from him and continue to make it the way he taught them. The two brothers now live about a mile west of the village, one right next door to the other. Luis makes Minero for Del Maguey, just like his father does, using a clay pot heated in a mud-brick stove. He buys maguey from his brother, a skilled farmer. Luis has inherited the style and flavor of his father's mezcal. His wife, Alejandra, works alongside him, one of just a few women who take part in production. His eldest son, Luis Jr., a veterinarian by trade, is being groomed as a palenquero, too. He gets tasked with the more grueling jobs, like punching down the cap of bagazo on the fermenting maguey mash. (In tequila, the spent maguey fibers are often removed for fermentation and almost always for distillation. To me, it's like removing the fat from milk or the germ from wheat—it's no longer whole, eroding not only the texture, but also nutrition.) Life on Luis and Alejandra's rancho is idyllic. Goats chew hay, chickens peck the ground, butterflies dance around wild rosebushes. There's nothing around but trees and maguey, a babbling brook, mountains in the distance. Even their outhouse is impeccable, a serene refuge. In the palenque, it's warm and sweet-smelling. Luis likes to throw a couple ears of corn onto the fire under the still. We peel back the husks and eat them hot and charred, no butter or salt. He does me the honor of letting me catch warm mezcal in an empty water bottle as it comes off the still. The first five hundred drops—*quinientos gotas*—are sacred. When we share a copita at the end of the day, his grandson, Joaquín, just a toddler, dips a finger in his grandfather's mezcal for a taste. Alejandra makes a show of chastising Luis for letting him.

Back at Don Lencho's home, his two daughters still care for their father. Neither has married. But a couple years back, one of the sisters, Elvira, experienced a miracle of her own. Whether she asked the Virgin of Juquila for it or not, I don't know. At the age of forty-five, she became pregnant and had a child, Emanuel. There is no father in the picture, but she doesn't seem to care. She's euphoric over the doe-eyed boy she carries with her everywhere, wrapped snugly to her hip in a thin-woven rebozo. The boy spends his days, like other Oaxacan toddlers, strapped to his mother, sleeping on her shoulder as she works, helping himself to her breast when he's hungry. Even before strangers, it causes her no embarrassment, just joyful laughter. Florencio seems to like the boy. I wonder if he'll manage to take him to the palenque and teach him a thing or two about his craft while he still can. I wonder what will come of that palenque, that living relic, when the old man is gone.

LUIS CARLOS VÁSQUEZ AND HIS WIFE,
ALEJANDRA, SANTA CATARINA MINAS.

LUIS CARLOS VÁSQUEZ, SANTA CATARINA MINAS.

DEL MAGUEY MINERO

SINGLE VILLAGE MEZCAL

Santa Catarina Minas, about an hour from the village of Chichicapa through a mountain pass, has an arid, semitropical climate and pristine water. Production here is carried out in the most ancestral way, the mezcal distilled in a pot made of clay with bamboo tubing, rather than the usual copper still. Despite the ancient process, these palenqueros are rather progressive: the palenque includes a cistern to cool and recycle the water used in the condensation process. Minero is warm and sweet. It has a nose full of flowers, vanilla, and figs, with a burnt honey note and whiff of lemon.

Production Notes

VILLAGE: Santa Catarina Minas

PALENQUEROS: Florencio Carlos Sarmiento, Florencio Carlos Vásquez, and Luis Carlos Martinez

STATE: Oaxaca

REGION: Valles Centrales

MAGUEY: Espadín (*Agave angustifolia* Haw.)

AGE OF MAGUEY: 8–14 years

ELEVATION: 5,052 feet (1,540 meters)

ROAST DURATION: 4–5 days

TYPE OF WOOD: Huizache, algaroble, plum, oak, zapote, jacaranda, mango, jarilla, araucaria, castor, pitayo, eucalyptus

MILLING: By hand

SIZE OF TINAS: 1,000 L

FERMENTATION DURATION: 15–25 days

WATER SOURCE: Well

STILL TYPE: Clay

STILL SIZE: 100 L

VOL ORDINARIO PER TINA: 170–210 L

ABV OF MEZCAL: 49%

VOL MEZCAL PRODUCED PER TINA: 30–70 L

DEL MAGUEY BARRIL

VINO DE MEZCAL

This special edition from our Vino de Mezcal series is made from semiwild barril—in other words, maguey that grows from seeds collected in the wild and planted in our fields. Barril are the biggest and fattest of the karwinskii subspecies, which includes tobasiche, madrecuixe, cirial, and larga. The mezcal has a nose full of carnations, gardenia, and jasmine, giving way to ripe pear, dark fig, and notes of damp green hay and forest floor. It enters the mouth like caramel, round and soft yet full-bodied. The long finish is reminiscent of roasted root vegetables and umami, leaving the mouth with a coating of terra-cotta minerality and a touch of salinity.

Production Notes

VILLAGE: Santa Catarina Minas

PALENQUEROS: Florencio Carlos Sarmiento and Florencio Carlos Vásquez

STATE: Oaxaca

REGION: Valles Centrales

MAGUEY: Barril (*Agave karwinskii*)

AGE OF MAGUEY: 18–30 years

ELEVATION: 5,052 feet (1,540 meters)

ROAST DURATION: 4–5 days

TYPE OF WOOD: Huamúchil, eucalyptus, oak, algaroble, plum, zapote, jacaranda, mango, jarilla, araucaria, castor, pitayo

MILLING: By hand

SIZE OF TINAS: 1,000 L

FERMENTATION DURATION: 30 days

WATER SOURCE: Well

STILL TYPE: Clay

STILL SIZE: 100 L

VOL ORDINARIO PER TINA: 170–210 L

ABV OF MEZCAL: 49%

VOL MEZCAL PRODUCED PER TINA: 40–80 L

DEL MAGUEY ARROQUEÑO

VINO DE MEZCAL

This special edition of 360 bottles is made from 100 percent semiwild maguey arroqueño. These giant, silver-hued plants have thin, spiky leaves. The mezcal shows a luscious ripe cantaloupe character and a hint of baking chocolate. Overall, it's vegetal and savory with a long, satisfying finish.

Production Notes

VILLAGE: Santa Catarina Minas

PALENQUEROS: Florencio Carlos Sarmiento and Florencio Carlos Vásquez

STATE: Oaxaca

REGION: Valles Centrales

MAGUEY: Arroqueño (*Agave americana* var. *oaxacensis*)

AGE OF MAGUEY: 12–25 years

ELEVATION: 5,052 feet (1,540 meters)

ROAST DURATION: 4–5 days

TYPE OF WOOD: Huamúchil, eucalyptus, oak

MILLING: By hand

SIZE OF TINAS: 1,000 L

FERMENTATION DURATION: 30 days

WATER SOURCE: Well

STILL TYPE: Clay

STILL SIZE: 100 L

VOL ORDINARIO PER TINA: 170–210 L

ABV OF MEZCAL: 49%

VOL MEZCAL PRODUCED PER TINA: 80–120 L

DEL MAGUEY PECHUGA

SINGLE VILLAGE MEZCAL

This traditional style of mezcal can only be made between November and January, when wild mountain apples and plums are in season. Pechuga begins with Minero mezcal, so it's already been double-distilled. A third distillation is carried out with wild apples and plums, other fruits and grains, nuts, and seeds, plus a whole chicken breast (or *pechuga*) suspended in the air of the still. Our Pechuga is bursting with aromas of basil, lemon, ocean spray, ripe fruit, and, yes, a hint of chicken. It's almost Scotch-like in its smokiness and brininess.

Production Notes

VILLAGE: Santa Catarina Minas

PALENQUEROS: Florencio Carlos Sarmiento, Florencio Carlos Vásquez, and Luis Carlos Martinez

STATE: Oaxaca

REGION: Valles Centrales

MAGUEY: Espadín (*Agave angustifolia* Haw.)

AGE OF MAGUEY: 8–14 years

ELEVATION: 5,052 feet (1,540 meters)

ROAST DURATION: 4–5 days

TYPE OF WOOD: Eucalyptus, huizache, algaroble, plum, oak, zapote, jacaranda, mango, jarilla, araucaria, castor, pitayo

MILLING: By hand

SIZE OF TINAS: 1,000 L

FERMENTATION DURATION: 15–25 days

WATER SOURCE: Well

STILL TYPE: Clay

STILL SIZE: 100 L

VOL ORDINARIO PER TINA: 170–210 L

ABV OF MEZCAL: 49%

VOL MEZCAL PRODUCED PER TINA: 70–80 L

DEL MAGUEY IBÉRICO

SINGLE VILLAGE MEZCAL

I worked closely with Chef José Andrés and his team at ThinkFoodGroup to create Del Maguey Ibérico, a unique mezcal distilled with Ibérico de Bellota, the legendary Spanish ham made using free-range, acorn-fed, black-footed Iberian pigs. Our collaboration began in 2012, when ThinkFoodGroup's research and development team, led by Chef Ruben García, came to visit the palenque in Santa Catarina Minas and witnessed the making of Pechuga firsthand. A couple of months later, he shipped a leg of Ibérico ham to me, and we soon began testing it out with our Pechuga recipe. The result is rich and meaty and endlessly nuanced.

Production Notes

VILLAGE: Santa Catarina Minas

PALENQUEROS: Florencio Carlos Sarmiento, Florencio Carlos Vásquez, and Luis Carlos Martinez

STATE: Oaxaca

REGION: Valles Centrales

MAGUEY: Espadín (*Agave angustifolia* Haw.)

AGE OF MAGUEY: 8–14 years

ELEVATION: 5,052 feet (1,540 meters)

ROAST DURATION: 4–5 days

TYPE OF WOOD: Huamúchil, eucalyptus

MILLING: By hand

SIZE OF TINAS: 1,000 L

FERMENTATION DURATION: 15–25 days

WATER SOURCE: Well

STILL TYPE: Clay

STILL SIZE: 100 L

VOL ORDINARIO PER TINA: 170–210 L

ABV OF MEZCAL: 49%

VOL MEZCAL PRODUCED PER TINA: 70–80 L

CHAPTER 6

INTO THE CLOUD FOREST AND BEYOND

The painter and caricaturist Miguel Covarrubias was from Mexico City, but became fascinated with southern Mexican tribal culture over numerous trips to the Isthmus of Tehuantepec. During his career, he contributed artwork to *The New Yorker* and *Vanity Fair*, and illustrated the books of his friends Zora Neale Hurston and Langston Hughes. But his great passions were anthropology and art history. In his 1947 book, *Mexico South: The Isthmus of Tehuantepec*, he chronicles the narrow stretch of land, a knot of jungle and brush, that links Veracruz and Oaxaca, touching corners of Chiapas and Tabasco. As the book's writer and illustrator, Covarrubias examines the history, art, folklore, and religious practices of the isthmus's indigenous tribes. Folded into the front of the book is an elaborately illustrated map depicting the area's mountain ranges, archaeological sites and holy places, and the traditional garb of various tribes—a woman naked from the waist up, another in an ornate huipil, another balancing a clay pot on the top of her head. Zapotec poets, he writes, loved to describe the graceful carriage of their women when burdened this way.

About a less-chronicled tribe, the Mixe (pronounced *MEE-hay*) of the valley of Oaxaca, Covarrubias says little is known. He describes them as "sturdy mountain people" and "primitive, shifting agriculturalists." Said to be descended from the Olmecs, the Mixe identify as Catholics, although their customs reflect a strong connection to pre-Columbian beliefs. He writes, "They bury their dead with a half gourd of tortillas . . . worship the spirits of lightning, of the earth, and of the clouds, to whom they make offerings of tamales, eggs, tortillas, candles of beeswax, incense, and the blood of turkeys and chickens, which they sprinkle on the earth to render it fertile or to make a boundary inviolable. The Mixe speak of whole towns of witches who turn into jaguars and snakes." A wild place, man.

In 1996, after the first cases of Del Maguey made it to the US, I got serious about searching out new mezcals to add to the collection. I went in search of a mezcal I'd heard of, from Santo Domingo Albarradas. The search took me to the border of Mixe country.

I borrowed the Bronco of my friend Pancho's brother and his father, Cosme, who'd been the one to tell me about this distant, magical village and its superb mezcal. Pancho, Cosme, and I rode together. We weren't prepared for what awaited us. I'd been used to driving along the potholed roads of Oaxaca. Desert mountains. The Sierra Madre. Cactus. Thorn trees. Maguey. But that's not all there is in Oaxaca. The state's landscape, like its people, is diverse. The drive took us up into an enchanted forest filled with wild maguey. The forest floor was covered in a spongy moss so green and clean it seemed artificial. AstroTurf. The trees, evergreen giants, were so tall their tops were out of sight. When Cosme and I first found ourselves in the thick of it, we slowed our

SANTO DOMINGO ALBARRADAS

DESTILACION

ESPIRIDIÓN MORALES LUIS,
SANTO DOMINGO ALBARRADAS.

vehicle to a crawl, craning our heads out the window to see where the fuck we'd come to. I had to stop and get out. The light was dappled through the hundred-foot-tall trees in an eerily beautiful way I'd never seen. The soft forest floor was pristine. The scene felt as though it were lit for a children's television show. I half-expected make-believe creatures to dance out from behind the ancient trunks. And it was quiet, as still as the inside of a church. I suppressed the urge to lie down and make the downy, cushioned ground my bed.

Cosme and I got back in the Bronco and continued our drive through the forest. We climbed up the mountain and saw that we'd entered a tropical microclimate. The air hung heavy and humid around us, the vegetation grew lush and exotic. Bromeliads grew in the forest on the pines. We left the paved road behind. After several hours of inching along a dirt trail at steep inclines, we came to the place where we could go no further. A large, white church stood overlooking a small village. In the distance, clouds hung at eye level, and I realized that the village sat perched over a wide gorge. Turkey vultures soared through the mist, low from our vantage, but a vast abyss yawned beneath them. The altitude here was some 8,500 feet above sea level.

We parked at the top of the village and walked down into it. The expressions on people's faces betrayed their surprise when they saw us. They were mostly subsistence farmers; they carried water around on burros. Few had ever traveled out of the region—other than those who left to find work—or welcomed visitors from afar. A gringo was unheard of, an alien. Cosme and I followed a cobbled road down to a little tienda that sold mezcal. The woman running the shop poured us a taste. The flavor was like the cloud forest itself—tropical, lush. We asked who the maker was and whether it might be the same person Cosme had heard of. It was. "Can we meet him?" we asked. "No," she answered. "He's out in the fields, on the other side of the river. An hour's walk." I told her I would be back in exactly one week's time. She assured me he would be there.

A week later, I made the five-hour trek once more—up into the enchanted forest, higher up still into the jungly mountains, over rocky roads, and to the big white church that overlooked the idyllic village of Santo Domingo Albarradas. I parked in its shadow, walked down the cobbled road to the shop, and announced myself. "I'm sorry," I was told. "He had to go get firewood," an errand that could take all day. I promised to return precisely one week later.

On my third trip to Santo Domingo Albarradas, I finally met Espiridión Morales Luis. He had a noble profile and sported a royal paunch. The nostrils on his nose flared, his neat mustache framed a Mona Lisa smile. His light-gray eyes shone. I recognized his soft-spoken sincerity expressed in the clean, honest mezcal he made. He was missing two fingers on his right hand, a childhood accident. He lost them when he was twelve, playing with fireworks, which also left him partially deaf. After the accident, he told his father he had trouble concentrating in school and asked if he could work in the palenque. Espiridión was suspicious of me when I first met him, unsure why anyone would come searching for him—especially a foreigner. I asked him to take me to his palenque and he agreed, reluctantly. A friend of mine later asked Espiridión what he thought of me that day. His answer surprised me: he was afraid, he said. Yet, he agreed to sell me some of his mezcal and we made an arrangement for me to become a regular customer. I started taking people to visit Espiridión and his family. I wanted people to see the incredible beauty and experience the vast remoteness of Santo Domingo Albarradas. Espiridión grew warmer toward me over time. His neighbors, however, continued to squint their eyes at my friends and me, full of skepticism, when we rolled into town. *Why were outsiders coming here now? How did they find us?* They were used to being isolated.

The visitors I brought were curious people. Bartenders and booze industry folk, they wanted to know Espiridión's secrets to making mezcal. How long did the fermentation take? How did he know when to cut the heads and tails during distillation? He was bemused by their interrogations. How did he know? He knew because he knew. How long did things take? Things took the time they took. He didn't analyze and fetishize the process the way his American visitors wished to. But one detail he was willing to expound on was the water. Espiridión uses water from a high mountain spring, and it's beautiful.

Every time I visit Santo Domingo Albarradas, Espiridión's wife, Rosa, prepares a feast. If it's a Sunday, they get special permission from the church to drink mezcal. This protocol suggests they would be conservative with the spirit, but they are not. He pours me a *mañanita*—the first copita of the day—that's a full three fingers. We'll drink like this until *la mañana* becomes *la tarde*. Rosa is one of the few palenqueros' wives who drinks with us. She is a sturdy woman with strong hands who helps out a great deal in the palenque. She cooks *chapulines* (grasshoppers), beans, eggs. On extra-special occasions, they roast a goat to flavor a rich soup. There are always oversize orange *criollo* (wild) corn tlayudas. I love to watch her working in the cook house, chickens pecking at the dirt ground at her feet as she toils over the wood-burning stove. Recently, I teased her, "We have a new palenquero, I see!" Her grandson, Sergio, used to run around the palenque, eager to help his dad and granddad but mostly getting in the way. Now, he leans against the fermentation tanks, arms crossed and barrel-chested, with an air of ownership. He's learning to do what his father and grandfather do.

One of the visitors Espiridión and his family welcomed repeatedly was my good friend Granville Greene. A journalist who specializes in outdoor adventure stories, he had approached me for a story he wanted to write about mezcal. He lived in Santa Fe, about ninety minutes from Taos, so we would see each other from time to time. His interest in mezcal grew, and he started traveling to Oaxaca whenever he could. He wrote a few articles about his travels with me. Eventually, he decided to turn them into a book. I put Granville up at Espiridión's, a base from which to conduct his research. He stayed in Albarradas for a while, watching and learning firsthand what life is like for a mezcal-producing family. I'd introduced him as "pueblo grande verde," the Spanish translation of his francophone name. They liked him and kept calling him that the length of his stay. Granville is an exuberant soul and an erudite son-of-a-bitch. One day, I drove in for a visit and found him with Espiridión's sons, thoroughly lit. They were all sitting around a half-empty gallon jug of mezcal, celebrating the completion of the last batch. Between giggles, they told me how Granville had wanted to help out in the palenque, so they assigned him the job of getting into the fermentation tank to scoop out the last of the maguey mash. He didn't want to soil his clothes, so he stripped down to his undershorts before getting in. Everyone at the palenque was doubled over in laughter at the naked gringo in the tank. They called the batch *mezcal desnudo*—naked mezcal—in his honor.

The first time I took Granville to Santo Domingo was the day after Día de los Taxistas in Oaxaca City. Yes, taxi drivers get their own day. They decorate their cabs with crepe paper and parade them through the streets. We'd gone to the Central de Abastos market in the town center that day so Granville could try pulque. I tried to explain to him how, even though pulque is a sort of maguey beer, its effects are totally different from those of mezcal. It's something you have to experience for yourself. We went to find the sisters, Hermanas Matteo, who sell pulque by the jícara. We bought one each and held the bowl up to our lips. Before taking the first gulp, I warned him, "You know, your eyes are gonna get all slitty. You're gonna get this tightness in the cheeks, like you can't stop smiling. The colors will get brighter. You'll see the world in a whole new way. Pulque is mildly hallucinogenic, man!"

I watched his high come on as mine did. We stumbled through the market, its sights and sounds amplified, then out into the streets. We made our way to the *zócalo*, the central plaza, floating along amid a sea of taxis all decorated with flowers and garlands, laughing like children, cheeks like apples, eyes wet with delight. It felt as though our minds had been blown wide open, the colors and music poured right in.

The next day, we left for Santo Domingo Albarradas before dawn, stopping in Tlacolula for a couple empanadas to sustain us during the trip. More than halfway there, driving slowly in fog as dense as bedsheets, Granville began to moan. He clutched his heart, then his left arm. "I think I'm having a fucking heart attack!" he cried. "We have to go back!" Uh-oh. I was pretty sure it was just indigestion, but you never know. I assessed where we were and patiently explained to him that it was too late to return to Oaxaca at this point. Albarradas was much closer. He started to panic. "Cálmate," I said to him. I'd seen my share of death. This wasn't it. "If you die out here, I promise to throw you the most spectacular funeral. I'll bring your parents out, too, so they can see the beautiful place where you met your end." He wasn't amused. Convinced his heart was exploding in his chest, he whimpered the rest of the way, his face pale and slicked with sweat.

We finally came out of the fog, and there was the white church. We'd arrived. A brass band was playing and fireworks were going off. It was the annual fiesta of the village's patron saint. Despite a light rain, everyone in town was out celebrating. All the jubilation was too much for poor Granville. We drove down to Espiridión's house and found his wife in the cook house. He's out, she explained, on some official duty as the head of the church committee in charge of the fiesta. Their son, Juan, came in and noticed Granville sweating, groaning, still clutching his arm. I caught Juan's eye. "Is there anything we can do for him?" I asked with a wink. "Yeah," he said, smiling. "Mezcal."

Juan poured us each a drink and there was Granville protesting. "I can't drink anything like this! I'm dying!" he wailed. "I need a doctor, not mezcal!" We urged him to take a sip anyway and, finally, he did. A moment later, his face changed. "How do you feel?" I asked him. "Better," he admitted. *Medicina.* After a couple more sips, he was fine and we all headed over to the fiesta to drink some more.

Para todo mal, mezcal. Para todo bien, también. ("For everything bad, mezcal. For all good, as well." One of my favorite *dichos*.)

In the twenty years since I first went to Santo Domingo Albarradas, little has changed. People are still religious, their customs and rituals the same mix of Catholicism and paganism they've practiced for centuries. They still live in simple adobe homes, eat simple home-cooked meals prepared from the vegetables they grow and the animals they raise. And yet, a lot has changed. Rosa's wood-fired kitchen now has a cement floor instead of dirt. People no longer carry water around on burros; it's now piped throughout the village from springs high on the mountainside. Espiridión has a big, new palenque with capacity for far greater volume than his old one. Since 2015, Chichicapa and San Luis del Río have had cell phones—one that each family shares—which makes communication with us so much easier and more efficient. No more five-hour drives to find that the man we've come to see is out fetching firewood.

The most important change is witnessed in Espiridión's children. His sons, Juan and Armando, have followed in their father's footsteps, making mezcal, rather than being forced to leave home to find work elsewhere. As Espiridión slows down—he's been making mezcal since the '50s and wore out his knees—Juan has assumed more and more responsibility at the palenque. He's being groomed to take over. His sister, Ester, has also joined the family business as the official secretary of Del Maguey's palenqueros. Another sister, Concepción, went to college, a first for the family. The two girls went to the city together, Concepción enrolling in classes while Ester cooked, shopped, and kept house in support of her sister. Concepción is now a lawyer in Mexico City. The entire village held a fiesta to celebrate her graduation. It brings me so much joy.

DEL MAGUEY SANTO DOMINGO ALBARRADAS

SINGLE VILLAGE MEZCAL

Santo Domingo Albarradas is located on the cusp of the Mixe region, a high-altitude tropical zone in the south of Oaxaca with a climate closely resembling parts of Hawaii. Tropical plants and fruits grow here beside rushing mountain streams. Cool, gray mists blow through valleys blanketed in pine tree forests. The mezcal is the fruitiest in the Del Maguey lineup, with a bright nose of citrus and roasted pear. Lots more tropical fruit comes through on the palate, giving way to spicy and woody notes, and, finally, a clean, dry finish.

Production Notes

VILLAGE: Santo Domingo Albarradas

PALENQUEROS: Espiridión Morales Luis, Juan Morales Luis, Armando Morales Luis, and Ester Morales Luis

STATE: Oaxaca

REGION: Valles Centrales

MAGUEY: Espadín (*Agave angustifolia* Haw.)

AGE OF MAGUEY: 8–10 years

ELEVATION: 4,855 feet (1,480 meters)

ROAST DURATION: 4–8 days

TYPE OF WOOD: Oak

MILLING: Wheel, horse

SIZE OF TINAS: 2,300 L

FERMENTATION DURATION: 10–12 days

WATER SOURCE: Spring

STILL TYPE: Copper

STILL SIZE: 350 L

VOL ORDINARIO PER TINA: 300–320 L

ABV OF MEZCAL: 48%

VOL MEZCAL PRODUCED PER TINA: 100–120 L

DEL MAGUEY SANTO DOMINGO ALBARRADAS TOBALA & ESPADIN

SINGLE VILLAGE MEZCAL

Espiridión and his sons, Juan and Armando, also make this blend of tobalá and espadín. The high elevation and cool, lush climate impart a rich mineral and herbaceous character to the mezcal. This expression is our first blend of two previously distilled mezcals: 58 percent tobalá and 42 percent espadín. We made this as a one-off and production is limited to 260 six-bottle cases.

Production Notes

VILLAGE: Santo Domingo Albarradas

PALENQUEROS: Espiridión Morales Luis, Juan Morales Luis, Armando Morales Luis, and Ester Morales Luis

STATE: Oaxaca

REGION: Valles Centrales

MAGUEY: Tobalá, Espadín (*Agave potatorum, A. angustifolia* Haw.)

AGE OF MAGUEY: 10–18 years

ELEVATION: 4,855 feet (1,480 meters)

ROAST DURATION: 4–8 days

TYPE OF WOOD: Oak

MILLING: Wheel, horse

SIZE OF TINAS: 2,300 L

FERMENTATION DURATION: 10–12 days

WATER SOURCE: Spring

STILL TYPE: Copper

STILL SIZE: 350 L

VOL ORDINARIO PER TINA: 300–320 L

ABV OF MEZCAL: 49%

VOL MEZCAL PRODUCED PER TINA: 160–200 L

SAN PEDRO TEOZACOALCO

As breathtaking and isolated as Santo Domingo Albarradas is, it's not the most remote village we work with. If a visitor is really game, I'll take them up to San Pedro Teozacoalco, a bucolic pueblo in a lush mountain valley in the Mixteca Alta region, which stretches from northeast Guerrero to the western part of Oaxaca. To get there, you have to drive hours on the worst dirt-and-rocks road I've been on. The rock face rising outside the car window shows striations. Deep red, then orange, white, black: different mineral compositions. You drive past a red lake, through a palm forest, and over a deep-blue river until you find yourself in old-growth forest. Fan palms stand next to pines. One day, I took Granville and another friend of mine named Tom to Teozacoalco. They wanted an adventure so we set out at five in the morning in my '85 Jeep Cherokee, taking a back route I'd never traveled. On the way, we pulled into a little village for breakfast. The road barely had room for a car. We came to a four-table café with an accordion roll-up door. The place was built over a raging river, in this incredible mountain canyon. Inside the café sat a parrot in a cage.

"What would you like?" asked the woman who owns the place once we were seated. I ordered *huevos revueltos con frijoles*. She brought me scrambled eggs with beans—and chicken. I didn't want chicken for breakfast! I began feeding the chicken to the parrot through the bars of the cage. The parrot was digging it.

"Where are you going?" the woman inquired.

"We're going to Teozacoalco," I told her.

"What for?"

"I work with a mezcal producer there."

"Oh! Do you know about San Jose Río Minas?"

They make mezcal there, she said. His name is Don Roberto. Granville went back to the Jeep to retrieve this old books of maps that contained every dirt road in Mexico. They don't sell these atlases anymore; they were invaluable in the days before GPS. We pinpointed Río Minas on the map and—holy shit!—it's the worst detour I've ever seen. The line representing the road is broken every quarter of an inch on the page: a treacherous drive.

"How's the road?" I asked the woman.

"Real bad."

"How many hours to get there?"

"Three."

I wished we had time, I told her, but we had to get to Teozacoalco and we still had eight hours to go. Next time. We left and drove on through the old-growth forest.

We reached the top of a mountain and up ahead saw four mountaintop villages we had to cross before we got there. Each one was down for an hour, then back up. The vista was dramatic, unspoiled. But monotony set in. After an hour or so, we came upon a barren plain strewn with giant black volcanic rocks. An hour and a half after that, we passed a lone guy pushing a bull up into the back of a pickup. At one point, we came to a place where a terrible storm had caused a mudslide and an entire village slid off the mountainside. Hundreds were killed. We saw steel doors leaning against trees where people were going to rebuild their homes. The local government had gifted them to residents.

We went on; the road split. There were no signs. We took the road going up and came to an old lean-to barn. *Shit*, I thought to myself. I had a hiker's compass in my glove compartment, the kind you pin to your shirt. I checked it. After five hundred feet, I said, "No, no, no. This is wrong." I turned back and took the other road at the fork. It took us down into a canyon where the fattest, greenest wild maguey I'd ever seen were growing out of the walls. We were in the zone.

All of a sudden, eight Indians with rifles planted themselves before our truck. Granville and Tom let out a scream. I rolled down my window and called out, "Hey! *Cómo se llama este maguey*?" What's that maguey called? The men in the road glanced at the plant I was pointing to, then back at me. One of them started walking toward the truck.

"You like maguey?" he asked.

"Yeah, man!"

"Where you going?"

"I'm going to Teozacoalco. I'm going to buy mezcal."

It was obvious to me that these guys were out deer hunting. They weren't dangerous, they weren't bandits. But Granville and Tom were terrified.

"Have you heard of Río Minas?" I asked. The man replied, "I'm Don Roberto, from Río Minas."

"No fucking way!"

Don Roberto addressed his friends in their indigenous tongue. One of them carried over a water bottle. I always keep two clay cups in the center console of my truck. I pulled one out and he poured me a sip.

"Man, I heard about you!" I said to him. "Río Minas is way over that way. How did you end up here?"

"We've been walking all day," he said.

"I love your mezcal," I told him and gave him my card. "Have you ever been to Teotitlán del Valle? You should come visit me sometime."

You don't find mezcal. Mezcal finds you.

FERNANDO CABALLERO CRUZ, OR AS
HE'S KNOWN IN HIS VILLAGE, SAN PEDRO
TEOZACOALCO, "EL BIGOTE."

Granville, Tom, and I continued on the road to San Pedro Teozacoalco. The producer I work with there, Fernando Caballero Cruz, makes mezcal from a variety known locally as *papalometl*: the butterfly maguey. It's like giant tobalá. Fernando goes by El Bigote because of the magnificent salt-and-pepper mustache he sports, a thick handlebar he twists into a curlicue at the ends. When I'd first heard about him, I tried reaching him by calling on the only phone in his village, the usual way to contact anyone in the remotest parts of the Oaxacan countryside. The person who'd answered told me there was no Fernando Caballero Cruz in Teozacoalco. I was forced to drive all the way out to look for him, not even knowing if he existed. When it turned out that he did, the explanation made me laugh: no one in his village knew his real name. They just called him El Bigote. The Mustache.

Bigote is a *cantador*: when someone dies, he is called to sing over the body, which is covered in cheesecloth to keep away flies, and has cotton balls stuffed into the nostrils. He sings to the gods to accept the departed soul into heaven. He's also a modern dude. A few years ago, he quit smoking. He also quit drinking and only takes his own spirit on the most special of occasions. Years ago, he woke up after a night of drunken antics on the sidewalk—the only stretch of sidewalk in Teozacoalco. Half his glorious mustache had been snipped off. Soon after, the sinner turned saint. Bigote has a green thumb and is proud of his orange and lemon trees. He serves squash blossoms from his garden when they're in season. Bigote's palenque is pristine. Wood stacked neatly, everything in its place. He set it up in an ingenious way that evacuates the smoke from the still fire through a rigged-up chimney. You can sit by the still all day breathing nothing but fresh air. He built the still himself, a stainless steel pot with a clay condenser and carrizo tubing. He used the *cogollo*, the bud at the center of the piña from which the quiote grows, to make a paste to seal the pot over the oakwood-burning fireplace. There are books and clean tasting-glasses on shelves in the palenque, in case anyone drops in for a visit.

When Tom, Granville, and I showed up, we found Bigote sitting in the palenque, looking out over his favorite mountain, a dormant volcano that looms in the distance. He welcomed us with a copita of his mezcal. Savory and earthy, it has an umami quality, like wild mushrooms. Granville and Tom were just beaming as we sat there with him, sipping and talking. They looked at me and shook their heads, as if to say, "*How? How did you* find *him?*"

A year and a half later, the office in Teotitlán got a call. A guy from San Jose Río Minas wanted to talk to me. Days later, Don Roberto showed up in a taxi cab, his mezcal in the trunk. He was nervous. A paranoia persists, especially in the remotest villages, about the government catching palenqueros with mezcal. Distilling was once a clandestine activity. Don Roberto had a twenty-liter plastic jug with him. It was the same remarkable mezcal I'd tasted in the lush canyon in the Mixteca. Don Roberto and I went straight to the bank in town so he could get paid. Showing typical Oaxacan hospitality, he invited me to stay with him in his village. Only, I wasn't alone. It was the day after the wedding of Maximino and Isabel, Faustino's son and daughter-in-law, in Chichicapa, and I had a group of guests, bartenders from the US, with me. Don Roberto extended the invite to us all. I gave the bartenders just one day to recover from the wedding, and then off we went to find Río Minas. I rented an SUV from Hertz at the airport big enough to fit seven passengers. When I went to pick it up, I couldn't believe my eyes. It was a solid gold Dodge Durango with bald tires and Mexico City plates. I filled it with gringos and we headed for the hills.

The road to Río Minas was as long as it had looked on Granville's map. We were on the road nearly ten hours total. In Río Minas, we found the main plaza where a big church overlooked the village and approached the only guy on the street.

"Don Roberto, *dónde está*?" I asked.

"Oh, he's out getting firewood. *Way* out there."

Shit. Nothing to do.

"Tell him Ron Cooper says 'hi.'"

All that way and we had to head home. On our way out of town, a woman started running after us, a hen tucked under her arm.

"I'm Don Roberto's wife!" she called out. She was followed by a beat-up red Chevy pickup. It pulled up alongside us and a young man leaned out.

"I'm Don Roberto's son, Alberto. Come with me."

We followed the pickup for an hour or so to this *pueblito* where maybe five or six families lived. We crossed a river on a suspension bridge made of chain-link fence and rebar. You looked out over the edge and saw the remnants of the last bridge, which was all rope. We had to get out of our vehicle and follow the road along the contours of the hills. On the way to the palenque, we passed a dirt plaza formed by three buildings, a thatched log cabin cook house, a one-room adobe house, and a newer one-room plaster and brick house. When we arrived, we saw a simple shelter with a long thatched roof that housed a rusty old still. Next to it were hollowed-out tree trunks for grinding maguey with wooden mallets. We sat outside at a table under a tree that had tools hanging from it, like a collection of artifacts. Simple, but beautiful. From that day, San José Río Minas became part of the Del Maguey family. Production is extremely limited, but the fact that the mezcal from this remote place makes its way to bars in New York or London is mind-blowing when you think of it. I'm sure it blows Don Roberto's mind, too.

CROSSING THE RIVER TO DON ROBERTO'S *PALENQUE*
IN SAN JOSÉ RÍO MINAS.

DON ROBERTO HOLDING A LEGAL,
VERIFIED SAMPLE OF HIS MEZCAL.

DEL MAGUEY SAN JOSE RIO MINAS

VINO DE MEZCAL

Made in the remote Mixteca Alta region, in the western half of Oaxaca, this mezcal is the perfect example of the dicho: "You don't find mezcal, mezcal finds you." Don Roberto's mezcal is bursting with bright, sweet aromas of papaya and ripe peaches. On the palate, it's soft and floral, a bouquet of roses and violets, with hints of pepper and *hoja santa* (in Spanish, "sacred leaf," an aromatic herb tasting of mint and anise that is only slightly carcinogenic), and a refreshing eucalyptus note that lingers on the finish.

Production Notes

VILLAGE: San José Río Minas

PALENQUERO: Roberto Gutiérrez Ramírez and Alberto Gutiérrez

STATE: Oaxaca

REGION: Mixteca Alta

MAGUEY: Espadín (*Agave angustifolia* Haw.)

AGE OF MAGUEY: 8–10 years

ELEVATION: 4,855 feet (1,480 meters)

ROAST DURATION: 3–4 days

TYPE OF WOOD: Oak, Tepehuaje

MILLING: By hand

SIZE OF TINAS: 220 L

FERMENTATION DURATION: 10–15 days

WATER SOURCE: Spring

STILL TYPE: Clay

STILL SIZE: 60 L

VOL ORDINARIO PER TINA: 30–40 L

ABV OF MEZCAL: 48%

VOL MEZCAL PRODUCED PER TINA: 12–15 L

WILD PAPALOME

VINO DE MEZCAL

San Pedro Teozacoalco is remote, to say the least. The trip takes hours on the worst rock and dirt road we have ever been on. The maguey Fernando Caballero Cruz uses, *papalometl*, is named for the Nahuatl word for butterfly (*papalotl*). It looks like giant tobalá. Fernando, known as El Bigote, distills in a small pot still with a clay condenser and carrizo tubing. The mezcal is earthy and dark, with a nose like sinking into a rich leather chair. There is leather, slate, and a hint of black olive and meat on the palate, with a finish of dried black cherries that gives way to savory mushroom.

Production Notes

VILLAGE: San Pedro Teozacoalco

PALENQUERO: Fernando Caballero Cruz

STATE: Oaxaca

REGION: Mixteca Alta

MAGUEY: Papalome (*Agave cupreata* × *A. potatorum*)

AGE OF MAGUEY: 10–12 years

ELEVATION: 5,200 feet (1,585 meters)

ROAST DURATION: 3–5 days

TYPE OF WOOD: Oak

MILLING: Wheel, Horse

SIZE OF TINAS: 220 L

FERMENTATION DURATION: 5–7 days

WATER SOURCE: Spring

STILL TYPE: Clay

STILL SIZE: 60 L

VOL ORDINARIO PER TINA: 30–40 L

ABV OF MEZCAL: 45%

VOL MEZCAL PRODUCED PER TINA: 12–15 L

ABOUT OUR BOTTLE LABELS

On the bottle label for San José Río Minas, a simple clay jug sits next to a humble home with a thatched roof. In the distance, ripe maguey sprouts from the hillside behind it. The drawing, like all our bottle labels and the cover of this book, is by the artist Ken Price, my good friend and former housemate in Ventura. Looking at it, you'd probably guess that Ken designed the label to depict places like Río Minas. But no.

When I first started Del Maguey, my plan was to feature a different artist friend of mine on each village's label. Art inside the bottle, art on the outside. My plan changed once I began leafing through Ken's drawings. I'd asked him to contribute something for one of the Del Maguey bottles and he gave me a stack of drawings he'd done in bed with his wife, Happy. "Take what you want," he said. I couldn't explain it, but it was like he had drawn all the places I'd been, even though I knew he'd never seen them. Kenny never went to Oaxaca. He must have walked through these places in his dreams. Santo Domingo Albarradas, Santa Catarina Minas, San Luis del Río—he captured them all so beautifully. Even now, I'll roll into a pueblo I've never been to and go, "Whoa! Kenny drew this twenty years ago!"

When Ken Price passed away in 2012, I was devastated. He was a great friend. Then it hit me: I might have to give up his sublime artwork. I didn't know how to approach his family about the drawings. They knew I loved Ken. But it was a delicate subject. I didn't want them to think I was worried about my bottle labels. I only wanted to honor his legacy and preserve the tradition we'd started together. Ken's wife, Happy, called me shortly after he died. Without my bringing it up, she told me to keep using the drawings, just as Ken would have wanted. I was moved by the gesture and pleased to continue having Ken's work conjure up the magic of Oaxaca. The bottles have become iconic. Bars and restaurants collect them, forming green-glass walls on their backbars. One bartender I met from Kansas City had the Chichicapa label tattooed on her arm. When I saw it, I thought to myself, "I bet Ken never could have predicted that."

CHAPTER 7

THE VILLAGE WITH NO NAME

When I was in art school, someone handed me a book—a weird, thin book, called *Mount Analogue*, published in 1952 by the French surrealist writer René Daumal. Part of the reason it was so thin is that it's unfinished. The author died young, before completing it. Tuberculosis did him in at the age of thirty-six. The book ends mid-sentence. The story is an allegorical tale about a mythical mountain that can only be perceived by those who climb it. Its peak, so high it's hidden, is said to link heaven and earth. Daumal was said to be an avid mountaineer. After reading this book, I started looking at my art in a new way. I began to take ownership of my artistic license in ways I hadn't before. Previously, I'd been bold, but always worked within a defined framework. Now, I began to map out my own rules for what it meant to be an artist. Later, when I found my own mythical mountain, I exercised my artistic license to give it a name. This mountain, just like Daumal's, can only be perceived by those who traverse it. I drove my pickup up into its enchanted forest and discovered that it was flush with tobalá. I didn't know the mountain's historical name, but I christened it Mount Tobalá.

In 1996, I was on my way to Santo Domingo Albarradas when I decided to take a short detour to Santa Maria Albarradas to find a mezcal maker named Rogelio. I was once again with Cosme, Pancho's father, who had heard about Rogelio and his phenomenal mezcal. We stopped by the palenque, at the foot of Mount Tobalá, and there he was: a slight, soft-spoken man with high cheekbones and a healthy glow about his skin. Big stars shining in his eyes. He stored his mezcal on the hill above his palenque. You had to go up through the village, past the old cemetery, the church, the municipio, and the market, and hang a right at the top of the village. He lived on one side of the road and he had this little red adobe two-room storage house across the street. Inside, the brick walls were red, the oilcloth tablecloth was red, the dirt floor was red. It was a funky little place. Rogelio poured us a taste of his mezcal. Cosme and I were blown away by it and each bought a liter. What Rogelio made was tobalá.

I had heard about tobalá before. There was an old mezcal maker, Adrián Sánchez, who I used to visit in downtown Tlacolula years back. He and his son ran a video store. On Sundays, we'd sit on the store's back patio and sip mezcal. He told me about tobalá, a mezcal that was hard to find because nobody wanted to make it. Working with this maguey made the skin itch, he said, and because it was so small, it took eight times more piñas to produce a liter than any other variety. He taught me the Zapotec meaning of the word tobalá. *Duub* means "maguey" and *bá alá* translates as "house" or "shade": the maguey that grows in the shade. I was intrigued. But I didn't get to taste tobalá just yet.

ROGELIO.

MOUNT TOBALÁ.

In 1990, when I made my first pilgrimage to the Virgin of Juquila, I went through Sola de Vega, a mezcal-making village. There I met Rodrigo, a dark-skinned Indian from the mountains. He just happened to be walking down the street with a jug in his hand on his way to the corner store near the municipio where he sold his mezcal. I stopped him and asked to taste what was in the jug. It was tobalá. Tasting it was transformative, like great art can be. It had a flavor that seemed to shift and stretch even as it sat in the mouth. It was earth and stones and sky and vegetation. I wanted more.

Rodrigo's palenque was between Sola de Vega and another village named San Andrés, along a sharp ridge. You took a winding path from the main road that linked the two and, suddenly, this long *llano*, a ledge jutting out like a finger, came out of the mountain. Along the llano were thatched-roof houses, burros, cornfields, maguey. It was the most stunning, primitive vision I'd ever seen. There wasn't a trace of the twentieth century in it. I felt I'd stepped into a premodern time, uncorrupted. I wanted to return to visit Rodrigo and buy more of his mezcal, but something stopped me. Crazy as it sounds, a few of the locals told me that brujas fly over San Andrés every Wednesday night. It scared me. I've learned to abide by the local superstitions in the villages. So far, it's served me well. Luckily, I found Rogelio. I didn't have to get mezcal from Rodrigo and risk encountering those brujas. Besides, Rogelio's tobalá was far superior to anyone else's.

I began visiting him regularly to buy his mezcal, twenty-five liters at a time—enough to share with my friends. It was more expensive than other mezcals, as most tobalá is thanks to the extra effort and material required to make it. Rogelio's total production couldn't have been much more than three hundred liters a year, so I was a good customer. I asked him to consider ramping up production so I could buy more and bottle it for Del Maguey. It was tricky, he explained. Tobalá was not like other maguey. The village government permitted producers to harvest it only one month out of the year to protect it from overharvesting. Most producers only made a few hundred liters a year, almost all of which was consumed during the village's annual fiesta celebrating its patron saint. What's more, Rogelio didn't have any sons or daughters to help him. But over time he agreed to increase his volume. And I was able to bring tobalá to the world.

This is something of a watershed moment for us. I've never revealed who my tobalá producer is or the village where his mezcal is made until now. Long ago, I decided to keep it a secret. Rogelio and his mezcal were just too special to advertise. And given the rarity of the variety and the local restrictions on harvesting it, I'd never forgive myself if word got out and the place got flooded with prospectors looking for wild tobalá. But I feel secure revealing it now. There was a time when I resented all the new brands entering the mezcal category. I had been the only one for so long. Suddenly all these new companies started coming into our villages, trying to poach our producers. In more than twenty years, no one has succeeded. So, I've mellowed. While it's true that certain brands are unscrupulous, I see now that the growth of mezcal as a category is a good thing. We are helping to create a new economy in Mexico. But I still have to protect places like Rogelio's village and its wealth of tobalá.

Of the two-hundred-plus varieties of magueys that grow wild in Mexico and the thirty or so that flourish in Oaxaca, tobalá is known as the king of them all. According to local legend, it was the first maguey, gifted to humanity by the gods, a distant ancestor of today's common varieties, like espadín and the karwinskiis. Biologically unique, it produces a complex and ethereal mezcal. Tobalá likes to grow at high altitudes, in the range of 7,000 to 8,000 feet above sea level. It thrives only in the shade of oak trees, like truffles. Driving through the mountains, I would always see this dwarf, broad-leafed plant clinging to rocky cliffsides and marvel at it. The plant's thin, shallow roots emit an enzyme that breaks down solid granite as it burrows into the earth in search of water and nutrients. Think of how grapevines absorb nutrients and minerals from the soil over their months-long growing season. Certain wines are said to express the minerality of their soils. Tobalá soaks up the earth's stony character for twelve, fifteen, even twenty years or more. That's how long it can take to ripen. Imagine the depth it possesses. Over its long lifetime, it doesn't grow large. Its average size is about eleven pounds, or five kilos, compared to, say, espadín, which can grow to two hundred pounds. In tobalá, the flavors and minerality are concentrated.

Tobalá is also rare because of how it reproduces. Other maguey varieties propagate both sexually and asexually. They sprout *hijuelos*—babies—which can be taken as cuttings and replanted. Tobalá does not produce hijuelos. It can only propagate through its sexual organ, the quiote, a thick stalk that emerges from the heart of the plant and can grow to more than twenty feet high. At the top, it sprouts tiny flowers that open at dusk, releasing their heady perfume to attract nocturnal pollinators, like bats and moths. These creatures help spread the tobalá's pollen, but the plant's survival rate is dismal. Given tobalá's preference for stony, shaded soils, seeds spread by the wind can land on rocks or shrubs, where they inevitably die. Those lucky enough to fall onto viable soil are vulnerable to nature's perils. Any that manage to become plants are small miracles. A tobalá that reaches maturity is a blessing.

Rogelio makes his mezcal with wild maguey from Mount Tobalá. He harvests the plants between ten and fifteen years of age and grinds them with a horse-pulled

ROGELIO POURING OUT
A *JÍCARA* OF HIS MEZCAL.

ONE OF ROGELIO'S HELPERS, REMOVING
BAGASO FROM THE STILL.

stone mill. He has no immediate family, but he doesn't work alone. He has a team of neighbors and nephews who help out. And, for some reason, he's always surrounded by women. I've never been able to discern if they're his friends, cousins, or concubines, but at least three of them have been with him for as long as I can remember. They take care of him, cooking and cleaning for him. These women have daughters and granddaughters, so he lives at the center of a fierce female circle.

It might explain his own energy, which is gentle and kind, yet extremely precise. He's quick to smile, but he's a serious person. Probably well into his sixties by now, he treads lightly on this earth, has a light touch—especially with his mezcal. It's beautiful to witness. The way he coaxes his horse around the molino is tender, the tip of a stick barely grazing the animal's hindquarters, Rogelio quietly clicking his tongue. After the horse's shift, it gets walked up the hill and hitched to a tree. The horse, sweaty from its work, takes a dust bath to cool off, rolling around in the dirt like a puppy before resting in the shade. Up the hill, by the side of the road, is where fresh piñas sit resting, waiting to be brought down to the molino. Rogelio has them piled underneath a huge, sprawling oak tree. A stunning sight to behold, it seems symbolic given how tobalá grows in the shelter of these trees. When it's time, Rogelio's helpers transfer the piñas to the palenque, where they get roasted, then crushed in the molino. The crushed maguey is fed into open wooden tanks. After a few days, water from a nearby spring gets added to the mash. The spring is known as Agua Santa: sanctified water.

Ten years ago, I took a group of bartenders down to Oaxaca and invited them to visit Rogelio. On the way there, the energy was high. We turned up the radio as my favorite song played. The honky-tonk legend John Prine, who'd worked as a postman to support his music, twanged in harmony with the folk singer Iris DeMent:

> *In spite of ourselves*
> *We'll end up a'sittin' on a rainbow*
> *Against all odds*
> *Honey, we're the big door prize*
> *We're gonna spite our noses*
> *Right off of our faces*
> *There won't be nothin' but big old hearts*
> *Dancin' in our eyes*

As we climbed out of the little tour bus I'd rented to get us around, the group grew quiet. They knew about the secrecy involved, having been instructed to keep their photographs of Rogelio and the palenque private. A sense of reverence hung in the air, and I could tell they were honored to meet my mysterious tobalá producer. Rogelio was sweet and welcoming, as usual. There in the palenque, surrounded by lush vegetation, a soft breeze on our skin, we all shared a copita of his mezcal together. As we basked in the quiet beauty of the place—and of Rogelio himself, whose eyes sparkled extra bright that day—one of the bartenders, Neyah White, spoke up.

"Those are roses growing over there," he remarked, pointing to a cluster of bushes nearby. I glanced around, searching the jungly green all around us and, sure enough, not fifteen feet from the stills and twenty feet from the fermentation tanks were about a dozen rosebushes in full bloom. We stood there, sipping our mezcal, looking from the roses to the tinas to the stills to our copitas and back again to the rosebushes, all thinking the same thing: *It's the roses.*

All Rogelio's mezcals have a delicate, floral quality. He's spry for his age and still loves to surprise me with new mezcals distilled from the wild maguey varieties he finds. He makes mezcal from tepextate, an overgrown dinosaur of a plant that produces a perfumed, candied mezcal. (When harvesting it, you have to shave it down to the white flesh of the piña so there's no green left whatsoever. With other varieties, the first couple inches of the leaf—the *penca*—can be left on the piña. It adds complexity to the mezcal. But with tepextate, the fibers are too bitter.) Rogelio also makes *jabalí* and a special espadín that we've named simply Espadin Especial. I always believed the pretty, ethereal aromas of these mezcals could be attributed to the light hand of the maker. But something else is at play, and it must have to do with the roses. The flowers' microscopic pollen gets carried off by bees, birds, and butterflies, deposited near and far. Does some of it end up in the ferment or in the stills? Perhaps. Might it influence the flavor of the mezcal? Quite possibly. The microclimate of that palenque, in that little closed valley, is intricate and complex.

Rogelio, like my other producers, has been able to make a couple of upgrades to his operation in the years since we started working together. Five years ago, he and his helpers moved the drainage system, which serves to remove the *vinasas*, or wastewater, that results from distillation, underground so that it wouldn't be muddy where they work. Two years ago, after expanding production to meet our growing demand, they raised the roof of the palenque to improve airflow. When Rogelio informed me that they would be replacing the old corrugated tar paper ceiling with new corrugated metal, which was more durable, I panicked.

"Don't change anything!" I pleaded. "It will change the mezcal!" I'd never been to Belgium, but I'd heard that the ceilings of lambic breweries are blackened from the airborne microbes that are necessary to ferment grains into sour, funky beer. Distilleries in Scotland and Kentucky have black mold growing on the walls, a fungus associated with the process of aging in oak barrels. Getting rid of these living microorganisms could throw off the entire ecosystem of those institutions. I'm no scientist. I've resorted to caution and superstition when it comes to our palenques. When Rogelio told me about his plans to upgrade the roof, I worried that modifying the environment in any way might impact the microbes embedded in the carrizo walls and the seams of the roof's panels. He assured me that it would be fine. And it was. The roof was changed and the mezcal stayed the same, still coaxed to life with the same ambient yeasts by the same maker's hand. Rogelio is a movable feast. Still, I wouldn't want anything else to change. The horse and the old molino. The piñas' resting place at the foot of the sprawling oak tree. The roses.

At home, I drink mezcal. I tend to go through phases—you could call them short-lived affairs—with different mezcals. I'll open a bottle from a producer we've just started working with or maybe something I haven't tasted in twenty years, and that's what I'll drink every day for a couple weeks or so. Then, once I've sat and chewed over every inflection and nuance, I'll move on to a new old friend. If every bottle and jug in my collection is a mistress, tobalá is my wife. I come back to it again and again. When I realize I haven't had it for a while, I instinctively know how many weeks or months have passed since I last did. When I taste it after a long absence, it's familiar to me, like home. But sometimes I'm struck by something that feels new, some barely perceptible subtlety I hadn't previously identified. For me, tobalá is the zenith, the quintessence of mezcal. It works to loosen the thoughts running around my head, allows them to settle and crystallize. Opens a path to wisdom, fuels the spark of new ideas. I've had incredible sculptures come to me in the dreams I dream after drinking mezcal. I believe it can open anyone's mind. But not everyone can do what I do. As I've said, this is my one true don, my god-given gift. You don't find mezcal, mezcal finds you. I don't show up to a village and taste every mezcal made there. I just happen to meet the one true artist, the best in the village. I've managed to forge relationships with the most genuine and honest people, the greatest craftsmen everywhere I go. My don led me to the best mezcal. My artistic license allowed me to name it.

THE KING OF MAGUEYS, TOBALÁ

DEL MAGUEY TOBALA

VINO DE MEZCAL

The tobalá maguey is found growing only in the highest altitude canyons, in the shade of oak trees, like truffles. Much smaller than other varieties, it has broad, flat leaves. Our Tobala is made in a mountainous, tropical microclimate. We keep our production limited and are careful to never overharvest the plant. The mezcal is sweet and fruity, with notes of mango and cinnamon, but also pleasingly herbaceous with a stony minerality. It is exceptionally nuanced and alluring.

Production Notes

VILLAGE: Santa Maria Albarradas

PALENQUERO: Rogelio Martínez Cruz

STATE: Oaxaca

REGION: Sierra Norte

MAGUEY: Tobalá (*Agave potatorum*)

AGE OF MAGUEY: 12–18 years

ELEVATION: 5,577 feet (1,700 meters)

ROAST DURATION: 30 days

TYPE OF WOOD: Oak

MILLING: Wheel, horse

SIZE OF TINAS: 1,400 L

FERMENTATION DURATION: 6–8 days

WATER SOURCE: Spring

STILL TYPE: Copper

STILL SIZE: 350 L

VOL ORDINARIO PER TINA: 100–220 L

ABV OF MEZCAL: 45%

VOL MEZCAL PRODUCED PER TINA: 80–100 L

DEL MAGUEY ESPADIN ESPECIAL

VINO DE MEZCAL

For fifteen years, our producer of Tobala wanted Del Maguey to bottle his espadín. At the insistence of a group of very special friends—dedicated bartenders, spirits educators, and connoisseurs—we finally did, but only as a limited-edition release. The first batch consisted of 330 bottles that were distributed in New York, Boston, and California. Since then, we've continued to bottle Espadin Especial and release it in select markets. The mezcal is deliciously floral with notes of vanilla, citrus, pineapple, and a hint of butterscotch, giving way to a mouthwatering saline quality on the finish.

Production Notes

VILLAGE: Santa Maria Albarradas

PALENQUERO: Rogelio Martínez Cruz

STATE: Oaxaca

REGION: Sierra Norte

MAGUEY: Espadín (*Agave angustifolia* Haw.)

AGE OF MAGUEY: 8–10 years

ELEVATION: 5,577 feet (1,700 meters)

ROAST DURATION: 7–15 days

TYPE OF WOOD: Oak

MILLING: Wheel, horse

SIZE OF TINAS: 1,400 L

FERMENTATION DURATION: 6–8 days

WATER SOURCE: Spring

STILL TYPE: Copper

STILL SIZE: 350 L

VOL ORDINARIO PER TINA: 200–220 L

ABV OF MEZCAL: 45%

VOL MEZCAL PRODUCED PER TINA: 100–120 L

DEL MAGUEY TEPEXTATE

VINO DE MEZCAL

Made from wild tepextate, a variety with broad, twisted leaves up to ten inches wide that grows at high altitude almost vertically out of rocks on the mountain face, this mezcal is delicate and ethereal. Candied fruit, banana taffy, and spun sugar blossom into passion fruit and marzipan. A hint of cinnamon lies in the background as a note of honeysuckle lingers on the finish.

Production Notes

VILLAGE: Santa Maria Albarradas

PALENQUERO: Rogelio Martínez Cruz

STATE: Oaxaca

REGION: Sierra Norte

MAGUEY: Tepextate (*Agave marmorata*)

AGE OF MAGUEY: 18–25 years

ELEVATION: 5,577 feet (1,700 meters)

ROAST DURATION: 15 days

TYPE OF WOOD: Oak

MILLING: Wheel, horse

SIZE OF TINAS: 1,400 L

FERMENTATION DURATION: 5–7 days

WATER SOURCE: Spring

STILL TYPE: Copper

STILL SIZE: 350 L

VOL ORDINARIO PER TINA: 200–220 L

ABV OF MEZCAL: 45%

VOL MEZCAL PRODUCED PER TINA: 60–80 L

CHAPTER 8

THE WOMB,
THE CONTAINER OF LIFE

/

THE SKULL,
THE CONTAINER OF LIGHT

Rodolfo Morales was a Zapotec painter from Ocotlán de Morelos, some thirty miles south of Oaxaca City, who became a famous artist. He left Oaxaca as a young man to take a job teaching art at a prestigious school in Mexico City, but was best known for the primitive, surrealist paintings he did featuring images of indigenous women. Near the end of his life, he returned to Oaxaca and took it upon himself to pay for the restoration of old churches in Oaxaca. One of these was Santo Domingo de Guzmán, a church and defunct monastery in his hometown. Constructed in stop-and-start phases beginning in the sixteenth century, by the nineteenth century, the church was in shambles and the monastery abandoned. In 1990, when I took my partner, Sandra, and her daughter, Ellen, there, the former monastery was being used as a prison.

The Santo Domingo de Gúzman prisoners were known in the region for the crafts they made and sold as a way to earn a meager living. I'd gone there to find out if they could weave baskets for my Ometochtli art project at a price I could afford. I envisioned the bottles, filled with mezcal, covered in handwoven baskets, just like bottles I saw in the market and the special wedding mezcal I received as a gift from Pancho's father. The three of us walked into the main courtyard. The walls housed grand vaulted arches. Iron jail cell bars had been affixed to these grand arches, the prisoners on the other side of them. At each one stood a guard carrying a Thompson submachine gun, the old Tommy guns from the gangster movies with the mahogany handle and the round-drum magazine that spat bullet casings like popcorn.

I approached one of the cells, Sandra and Ellen behind me, and showed the prisoners a classic Coca-Cola bottle I had with me. This was the original Raymond Loewy–designed bottle with the cork stopper. I explained that I wanted to fill something like it with mezcal for an art project and asked if they could weave a basket to fit the bottle like a glove. They were amused. One of them called himself El Tigre de Santa Julia, after the famous old *bandolero*, Mexico's answer to Billy the Kid. He said he would do it. I asked how much he would charge me. He got quiet and beckoned me closer to the cell. Glancing sideways at the guards, I took a step forward. "We want mezcal," he whispered through the bars. I gave a subtle nod. We had a deal. A couple weeks later, I returned to the prison, little plastic baggies filled with mezcal hidden inside my shirt. Without even looking at the guards, I went right up close to the cell bars to get my woven baskets from El Tigre. Silently, I slipped the baggies through the bars and quickly departed. He and his cellmates were as giddy as school kids.

Dealing with the prisoners of Santo Domingo de Gúzman was cool, but it occurred to me that it might not be the most sustainable working relationship. I remained on the lookout for basket weavers to collaborate with. At the time, on days when I wasn't working on art or out on the road in search of mezcal, I enjoyed going to the Mercado Benito Juárez, below the zócalo in Oaxaca City. The market is a cacophony for the senses. Rows upon rows of stalls, it takes up a full city block and spills out onto the bordering sidewalks and streets. Inside, the sights and smells are overwhelming: piles of ripe produce, raw meat and sausage links hanging from hooks, wide trays heaped with brick-red roasted grasshoppers, every manner of dried chile, vats of mole (all seven colors, from *amarillo* to *negro*), breads, cheeses, fresh-caught fish, plus huaraches, sombreros, and touristy gifts like cheap textiles and mezcal with a worm at the bottom of the bottle.

The market, like so many things in Oaxaca, is named for Mexico's first indigenous president. Benito Juárez, who served from 1858 to 1872, was a Zapotec Indian, orphaned at an early age and raised in poverty by a negligent uncle in the village directly above Teotitlán del Valle. He went on to become a world-famous progressive reformer and one of the country's most beloved leaders. He vehemently rejected the Catholic church and the colonial system it perpetuated. Instead, he pushed for a liberal, secular, and market-driven society. The bustling market named for him is a testament to his legacy.

Most days, seated on the ground just inside the eastern entrance of the market amid the beautiful chaos of the place, were a group of women weaving baskets out of palm fiber. I would stop near the women regularly to watch them. One day, I brought a Coke bottle full of mezcal with me. "Hey, can you weave around this?" I called over to them as they worked. They said they could. I told them, "I'm working on this art project and I'd love to collaborate with you. What you do is the most beautiful art form, the most ancient. It's older than pottery. Can we work together?" "Yeah, sure," they said.

I became friends with the women, visiting them often at the market. Several years later, when Del Maguey was getting off the ground, I arranged to meet them in their village. I drove the three hours out to Miahuatlán, due west of the city, to visit the basket weavers on their home turf. The women were sweet with me, but when it came down to talking shop, they were the toughest businesspeople I'd ever encountered. The entire village gathered when I arrived. Just about every woman in the village makes baskets for a living. I presented my request to them, that they make baskets for my mezcal bottles. They agreed and went on to appoint a president, secretary, and treasurer to lead the committee in charge. To this day, I work with these women.

A couple years ago, I learned that twenty-six of the forty-seven women from Miahuatlán were heading up to Sonora to plant crops. Ana, the leader of the village committee in charge of weaving for us, admitted as much to me when none of the

others would, her mother, Inés, who I'd known since 1985, included. The women had decided to plant crops because they were too proud to ask for more money from Del Maguey. As soon as I found out, I arranged for a raise. Immediately, the women started coming home. Del Maguey later established two funds for the weavers, one to support the women's health care and another for their children's education.

I still like to watch the women from Miahuatlán as they weave. Watching them work, I've developed this theory. It's about how language was born. Museums tend to showcase hard tools, axes and spears, as evidence of early civilizations. But I believe advanced culture began with baskets made of dried reeds. I believe it was women, like the weavers of Miahuatlán, who invented language in prehistoric times. All the men had to do was hunt. Sitting out in the woods, waiting for an animal required quiet. But the women had to gather. And for gathering, they needed vessels. Sending a daughter afield to gather nuts, seeds, roots, bark, and fruits required the communication of abstract concepts. *Go over that mountain, down that river, to the big tree at this full moon.* Such specificity required language. It was communal, the sitting around and weaving of baskets, just as it is now. From primitive words, women developed a sophisticated way of talking with each other that persists today.

As civilization evolved, so did vessels. Humans learned to form and then fire clay. The first pots used for storing food and water probably date to 10,000 BCE. When I started looking for a vessel I could use for tasting mezcal, I settled on clay, an organic material. I wanted to mimic the traditional vessel used to taste mezcal, the jícara, a thin-walled, hollowed-out gourd sometimes decorated with etchings on the outside of the bowl. As a material, the gourd skin is porous, it breathes. When you pour mezcal into it, the jícara drinks its share. Over time, the mezcal cures the bowl, but the bowl imparts nothing to the spirit. When you bend your face to it for a sip, you're enveloped by aromas from the mezcal. There is no intense alcohol burning your nose, just the smell of roasted maguey, mineral, fruit, flower overtones.

I met the Benítez family in the Central de Abastos market, where I've found so many treasures over the years. They were selling their pottery, which they make on Cerro del Fortín. It's the hill overlooking Oaxaca where the traditional dances for the annual Guelaguetza festival are held. (Guelaguetza, held on consecutive Mondays in the second half of July, celebrates native culture through costume and dance. The event is ancient, with roots in pre-Hispanic sacrifices offered to the god of corn. The word *Guelaguetza* comes from the Zapotec for "exchange of gifts"; the dances performed are considered offerings from one tribe to another.) I once saw a photo of the Cerro del Fortín from the 1930s or '40s: there were no roads. Just old cars and people scattered like ants across the hillside. The Benítez family has made pottery there for generations. I worked with them to design a copita that, like the jícara, would breathe. We worked on the shape, which has morphed slightly over the years, but is basically a squat cup that stands roughly an inch high. It holds a perfect measure of mezcal and sits comfortably in the hand. It's the perfect size for hiding in your pocket. I always carry mine in my jeans or my jacket—you never know when someone will want to pour you a nice mezcal. No one has ever been able to shape the copitas like the Benítez clan. The family's old *abuelo* passed away a while back, but I remember him clearly, leaning against a wall before his wheel, kicking a four-foot-tall volcano of clay around and around, shaping copitas by the hundreds per day.

The copitas have taken on a life of their own. I've read misguided articles that claim they are traditional Oaxaca artifacts. They are not. They're all me. They were invented out of necessity, but I'm always pleased when a bar or restaurant wants to use them for serving our mezcal. When people come to visit me in Oaxaca, I give them a copita and make a little drawing on the foot of it for them. It's my way of saying thank you.

As I've mentioned, vessels are a recurring theme in my art. In my early works, they held water. I've always found water to be a beautiful and powerful element to work with. In later works, my vessels held mezcal, the sacred juice. The vessels were like goddesses: the womb, the container of life. Mezcal was the food, feeding the skull, the container of light. For me, a work of art is successful if, in the making of it, a question is generated. The answering of that question becomes the next work. The sculpted vessel led to the liquid contained therein; working in the avant-garde led me to the ancient. I've always liked a passage the writer and mythographer Marina Warner wrote in a 1991 essay for the art magazine *Parkett:* "The beast within begins to look like a sign of grace compared to the vices and disorders of industrial man." It's about finding peace and salvation in the primordial, taking

DEL MAGUEY'S CLAY *COPITAS.*

154 refuge from the dysfunction of modernity in the primitive. Embracing the ancient has allowed me to pursue the progressive unencumbered by its dogma.

I used to be a very private artist. I worked in archetypes and metaphors. I hung out in my studio, napped on my couch. I swept the floors. I worked alone. I had a linear process. I went from Point A to Point B to Point C. Order was my religion. I'd work until four, five, six o'clock in the morning, around the clock for three days straight. Then I'd rest. I made my art, hung it in my studio, looked at it, moved it to a better spot, looked at it some more. Sometimes I went to art openings or other social events, or had curators visit. But that was it. That was my life. My responsibility was for myself and my work. I took care of my family, enjoyed the company of friends. But it was a small life. Now, life looms large. My extended family has swelled to include a dozen mezcal-producing communities, another dozen guys who work in the *bodega* (our office, bottling, and storage facility), 150 women in Miahuatlán, and the family that makes the copitas. I get to participate in the interconnectedness of people. I do my part to preserve an ancient way of life.

I still work in archetypes and metaphors, but I am grateful to have been introduced to a culture that maintains a primal closeness to ancient divinity. Making mezcal is a craft and a livelihood, but it is also a rich celebration of life and an expression of holy devotion. My producers, several of whom allow the spirit to touch their lips but once a year, tell me this all the time. When I ask, "Why do you make mezcal?" They answer, "Because it brings us closer to God."

DEL MAGUEY BODEGA ALTAR, DÍA DE LOS MUERTOS.

CHAPTER 9

A POUND OF FLESH

Dear Mr. Cooper:

This concerns the claim to copyright in the work entitled
EIGHT AND ONE QUARTER INCH SPHERICAL VOLUME
OF ATMOSPHERE.

Since the material you have submitted does not contain any matter
subject to copyright, registration is not possible.

Sincerely yours,
Dorothy M. Schrader
Head, Arts Division, Examining Section
Library of Congress, Copyright Office

This letter was part of a correspondence with the Office of the Register of Copyrights that I carried on in 1969 in the name of art. I had tried to register an eight-and-one-quarter-inch sphere of air at specific latitudinal and longitudinal coordinates: North 34.0220, West 118.1607. The written exchange itself was the piece. It was about the nature of art, the disruption of establishment. I wanted to pose the question "Why can't this spherical volume of atmosphere in my studio on Figueroa Street (now under the Staples Center) in downtown LA be art? Why can't I claim empty space as my own?" It was a conceptual work and turned out to be an exercise in the futility of dealing with bureaucracies. I was reminded of this piece during the process to get Del Maguey's producers certified under what was then known as COMERCAM: Consejo Mexicano Regulador de la Calidad del Mezcal. Today, it goes by the abbreviated CRM: Consejo Regulador del Mezcal, or the Mezcal Regulatory Council.

Mezcal, like tequila, is protected by Mexican and internationally recognized law. In 1994, it earned a *denominación de origen*, or DO, a status like that assigned to Champagne, Cognac, and Scotch that identifies it as a culturally and geographically distinct product. In Mexico, the status is outlined in a *Norma Oficial Mexicana*, or NOM. NOMs are Mexico's official standards for everything from commercial product manufacturing to health-care practices. Tequila got its NOM in 1974, so it had a twenty-year jump on mezcal. Awarding mezcal the same status as tequila was supposed to protect mezcal makers from counterfeiters, enforce standards of quality, and ultimately help promote the spirit on a global stage. Unfortunately, because mezcal's NOM, NOM 70, was virtually copy-and-pasted from tequila's, it failed to protect producers from the greatest danger: losing their culture.

Tequila's regulations, unlike those for Champagne, Cognac, or Scotch, do not specify how the spirit should be made. They only state that the spirit must be made from cooked blue agave that's been fermented and then distilled twice. The methods for cooking, crushing, fermenting, and distilling are not stipulated. This is why, in tequila, traditional brick ovens have been replaced by pressure cookers called autoclaves (and worse, the behemoth machines known as diffusers that process agave using hot water and chemicals without cooking it at all). The *tahona*, tequila's word for "molino," has all but disappeared, replaced by mechanized shredders borrowed from the rum industry, where they're used to grind sugar cane. Fermentation is carried out by inoculating agave sugars with synthetic or lab-bred yeasts. When the rules for mezcal were first established, traditional hand-harvesting methods, the use of underground hornos, molinos, tinas, and even copper or clay pot stills were equally left out of the legalese. Instead, it was stipulated that mezcal could consist of up to 20 percent unnamed "other sugars," like tequila's 49 percent allowance for sugars not derived from agave (usually corn- or sugar cane–based), which was put in place to offset agave shortages in Jalisco. Few mezcal producers made the 20/80 *"mixto"*—it was not economical—although plenty adulterated their product. Recently, regulations have changed.

One of the biggest problems with NOM 70 was a restriction on acetic acids, one of the most important flavor components in mezcal (and wine and other spirits). Acetic acids occur naturally in many fruits and vinegar; they cause you to salivate, sparking your appetite. They're necessary for balance in a wine, whiskey, or mezcal. Prescribing an arbitrary ceiling on these acids can throw a spirit off balance. Another problem with NOM 70 was its geographical limitation. It applied only to producers in five states: Durango, San Luis Potosi, Guerrero, Zacatecas, and Oaxaca. But mezcal is made in just about every state in Mexico. Producers around the country, mostly Indians and mestizos from the poorest parts, were excluded. Instead, they've been forced to call the liquid their families have made for generations *destilado* (distillate) or aguardiente. The reason for controlling the use of the term *mezcal* is purely economical. Big brands want to capitalize on commercial recognition of the word and prohibit small producers from using it. In recent years, the tequila and mezcal industries have tried to tighten this stranglehold by proposing new laws and NOMs that would restrict how agave spirits are made and marketed. They've sought to limit the use of not only the word *mezcal* but also *agave*. Preposterous. It's like trying to restrict the use of the word *grape*.

These latest attempts to stifle the smallest producers with red tape and arbitrary regulations were met with resistance. In late 2011, NOM 186 sought to restrict the use of the word *agave* on bottle labels, while an accompanying proposal aimed to copyright *agave*. Del Maguey sent out a heads-up to bartenders and consumers worldwide, and many signed petitions criticizing the proposed regulations, pressuring the regulatory bodies involved to reconsider their actions. NOM 186 was defeated. Then, in 2015, NOM 199 threatened to impose a new classification on producers outside the existing DOs for tequila and mezcal. Their mezcal was to be reclassified under the vaguely indigenous term "komil," a word no producer had even heard of. More petitions were circulated and that proposal too was ultimately defeated. In both cases, the petitions cited evidence from Mexican academics and testimony from the producers themselves, but it was the influence of thousands of consumers worldwide that made the greatest impact. Their purchasing power gave them a voice. The mezcal NOM is an imperfect system designed with an eye to the global market, the original regulations shaped by chemical engineers and corporate executives to sell mezcal to the world. But when the world starts standing up for small producers and demanding more transparency from corporations, the system can be disrupted. I was proud that so many consumers and bartenders who were introduced to mezcal through Del Maguey took up the fight.

A few years ago, the process to overhaul NOM 70 was initiated. The new NOM went into effect in 2017. It now recognizes artisanal and ancestral methods of production and requires mezcal to be made from 100 percent maguey. No more mixo. It also bans diffusers, large machines that process raw maguey using hot water and sulfuric acid, as a cooking method. It's still imperfect—in their eagerness to acknowledge traditional methods, the authors of the new regulations have allowed for certain producers who fall outside strict definitions to be pigeonholed. For example, palenqueros who use makeshift stills that aren't made of clay cannot qualify as "ancestral." Mezcal makers are creative, clever people. I've seen many improvisations in palenques around Mexico, handmade stills that have been in use for generations cobbled together from repurposed materials. Telling these producers their methods are less than ancestral doesn't sit well with me or them.

Today, there are nine states protected by NOM 70. Over the years, municipalities in Tamaulipas, Michoacán, and Guanajuato were inducted—and Puebla. When I first went to the state of Puebla, it was not yet part of the NOM. The decision to work with the producers I met there came with the assumption that I'd have to bottle their mezcal as "destilado." *Espirituosa de Puebla*, read the bottle label I had designed. In the US, I was forced to go through the process of getting a new spirit approved by the Alcohol and Tobacco Tax and Trade Bureau, the TTB. Puebla could not come into the country as a mezcal, so I had to start the approval process from scratch. Dealing with the TTB's bureaucracy was a headache. Then, just as Espirituosa de Puebla was about to get the green light, the state of Puebla was inducted into NOM 70. All that paperwork for nothing. No matter. Del Maguey ended up being the first to sell a mezcal from Puebla in the US.

To get to Puebla from Teotitlán de Valle, you have to pass through Nochixtlán in northern Oaxaca, the site of the deadly teacher protests of 2016. The teachers have been taking over central Oaxaca in protest each May for as long as I can remember. In 2016, the Mexican government proposed education reform measures that were especially inflammatory. The plan to impose standardized testing for teachers and remove job protections was similar to reforms that have been proposed in the US. In Mexico, it had teachers up in arms and everyday citizens conflicted. Teachers are the highest-paid public employees in the country, and their union is one of Latin America's most powerful. People want their children to get a good education, but find themselves resenting the *maestros* and *maestras* their preferred status.

The summer the teacher protests turned grizzly, nine people were killed by police and dozens more wounded. Nearly two months had passed by the time I drove through Nochixtlán. I slowed my vehicle down to rubberneck the still fresh-looking carnage. The rusting skeleton of a burned-out bus was lying on its belly in the middle of the main road out of town. The burned carcasses of a couple of other cars had been abandoned on the shoulder. I spotted a few Mexican tourists taking selfies with the bus, which still bore a white banner that read *Asesinos del Pueblo*: culture killers.

I was in the pickup with Arturo Ramirez Zenteno, our head of quality control. Arturo, a Puebla native, is a chemical engineer. He'd worked at the Mezcal Regulatory Council for several years before getting a job at Casa Armando Guillermo Prieto, a huge distillery that manufactures industrial mezcal. Several changes in management and poor sales led the company to make cuts to its staff. Arturo found himself without a job. He was friends with one of the guys in our bodega who ended up telling me about Arturo. I was intrigued. We met and I offered him a job on the spot. Arturo is soft-spoken and kind with a shy, cherubic face. Since joining Del Maguey, he has become invaluable to us. He tastes every batch of mezcal from each one of our producers before it gets bottled. His palate is practically infallible, his scientific mind sharp. And he's able to communicate with the producers like no one else can. They feel as though Arturo understands them. They share hopes and concerns with him that they would prefer to keep from me and jokes I'm not always privy to. Arturo has become my right-hand man. My pistolero. He is the one who goes with me on my adventures now.

MEZCAL'S REGULATIONS

A few years ago, a process to overhaul NOM 70 was initiated. The new regulations went into effect in 2017. The most significant change is the abolition of "Type 2" mezcal or *mixto*: all mezcal must now be made with 100 percent maguey. The new NOM also makes no mention of permitted varieties, as the old one did. And it bans the use of diffusers, large machines that process raw agave using hot water and sulfuric acid, as a cooking method (although they are permitted for grinding maguey).

The other major change is a breakdown of the mezcal category into three subcategories:

Mezcal should be made using maguey that's been cooked in an underground conical oven, brick oven, or autoclave; ground in a stone mill or in a mechanical shredder or with a diffuser; fermented in wood, concrete, or stainless steel tanks; and distilled in a pot or column still.

Artisanal mezcal should be made with maguey that's been roasted underground or steamed in a brick oven; crushed by hand, stone mill, or mechanical shredder; fermented in stone, earth, wood, clay, or animal-skin receptacles with the bagazo (spent maguey fibers); and distilled with bagazo in a copper or clay pot still over a wood fire.

Ancestral mezcal must be made with maguey roasted underground; crushed by hand or in a stone mill; fermented in stone, earth, wood, clay, or leather receptacles with bagazo; and distilled in clay pots with bagazo.

Being that Arturo is from Puebla, I had repeatedly urged him to check out the mezcals from his home state. When he finally brought me some samples and I tasted them, I knew I wanted to bottle a mezcal from Puebla for Del Maguey. But it took nearly a decade for me to find a producer I wanted to work with there. The mezcal that did it was a sample Arturo shared with me from San Pablo Ameyaltepec, a village about twenty-five miles from his parents' house in San Vicente Coyotepec. The time had come for us to set out on an adventure together.

Sunday is market day in Ixcaquixtla, about a fifteen-minute drive from San Vicente. Merchants from Ameyaltepec bring their mezcal to sell there. Arturo was nervous. This was his first long-distance trip as the driver of a Nissan 4x4 Del Maguey had purchased for him. Before then, he didn't drive. He took buses to travel to the six different villages he visited each week in Oaxaca to carry out his quality control and compliance duties. He also traveled by bus back to Puebla. Arturo had also never hunted for mezcal before, which added to his jitters. What if we did not find any that was good enough? I tried to calm him through distraction. From the truck, I began pointing out the wild maguey growing on the hillsides around us—tobalá, tepextate. We later learned that, in Puebla, these went by different names: *papalote, pizorra.*

We found ourselves in a fertile valley with a semitropical climate. Fields of *calabaza* (squash) and plots of other vegetables surrounded us. Iztaccihuatl and Popocatepétl, two volcanic peaks (one dormant, the other not) loomed to the north, toward Mexico City, smoke rising from the latter. A rough, unpaved road took us into San Pablo Amayeltepec. We asked around for a woman known for bringing the village's mezcal to the weekly market in Ixcaquixtla. She was nowhere to be found. Instead, we met an old guy who traded wild maguey to palenqueros for finished mezcal. I asked if he had any on him and he took off in his pickup, returning a few minutes later with a twenty-liter plastic container, called a *cubeta*. We asked if there were other producers whose mezcal we could taste. He pointed to a tiny corner store run by an ornery old woman. There was barely enough space inside for me, Arturo, the woman, and the mammoth Coke machine she kept in the room. We whipped out our clay copitas and she poured us some really good local stuff from a plastic water bottle. Several guys came in from working the fields and bought Cokes to take out front as we finished our *mezcalitos* (little mezcals) inside. We asked the woman if there was a palenque nearby we could look at. "Yes," she said curtly. "Right around the corner and downhill a block."

The palenque was dark and warm inside. Not daring to go in uninvited, we peered into the spaces between the rustic planks of the walls to see into this funky little place. The smoke from the wood-burning still stung my eyes. The still was a sort of hybrid I'd never come across before, although I would see it again in other palenques in Puebla. The *cabeza* (head) of the typical Amayeltepec still contains three flying saucer–shaped plates so that it acts like a continuous still. The plates capture high alcohols, while the lesser vapors fall back down, separating the heads from the heart from the tails again and again. In other words, it can distill multiple times during a single run, like an Armangnac still, allowing the producers to make great mezcal with a single distillation.

Suddenly, a man showed up and introduced himself as Aurelio González Tobón. He said he was the one making mezcal inside at the moment, but that the palenque was shared among five producers. Aurelio invited us in and showed us around, introducing us to the other palenqueros. Working with neighbors brought them joy, he explained. Later, he took us to his house a little way uphill to taste his mezcal. He poured from three one-liter soda bottles that sat on the floor of his bedroom. The mezcal was exquisite. Each was made with the local papalote variety (known elsewhere as tobalá). Aurelio had a special mezcal distilled with meat and fruits that I can only describe as tasting of liquid mole. I bought whatever he had to sell. He told us about how he'd just moved back home from the city where he'd been the driver for the governor's office. His kids were grown and city educated, his wife had ended her teaching career. After many years in the capital, his village called to him. He longed to make mezcal like his father.

On our next trip to San Pablo Amayeltepec, we stopped in to visit Arturo's family in San Vicente Coyotepec. His mother and sisters-in-law laid out a barbacoa feast for us, a poblano specialty, with all the fixings: smoky slow-cooked sheep meat, avocado and tomato salad with chopped cilantro, homemade salsa, frijoles and tortillas, and cold beer. His twin nieces and nephew watched us as we ate, politely answering all our questions. (When we first arrived, they greeted each of us with a courteous handshake. I've become accustomed to this behavior among children in Mexico and often find myself put off by American kids who can be so shy it's tedious or the opposite: they completely ignore adults.)

Arturo's father, Cristóbal, tended the little store at the front of the house and poured me a copita of the fine mezcal served at Arturo's wedding a few years back. It was soft as a whisper yet showed the rich complexity of a mezcal that's been left in a bottle for a few years. Aged in glass, they call it. *Añejado en vidrio*. That, too, is recognized in the new NOM regulations and something I've advocated for twenty-seven years, that good organic mezcal matures in glass, developing and deepening.

AURELIO GONZÁLEZ TOBÓN AND HELPER
RETURNING FROM HARVEST OF MATURE PAPALOTE.

Arturo and I left his parents' home full-bellied and headed for Aurelio's. As soon as we arrived, his wife, Sonia, tried to usher us inside for a meal. Not wanting to disappoint her, I suggested we visit the palenque first while we still had daylight. (Mostly, I wanted time to digest the feast we'd just been fed.) Del Maguey had underwritten a brand-new palenque for Aurelio, which had yet to be unveiled. Several other mezcal producers in town wanted to show us their facilities, too. We took a little tour. Before heading back for dinner, we paid a visit to Aurelio's father's rickety old palenque. The walls and ceiling were cured a deep maroon, like dried blood, from the decades of smoke wafting up from the wood-fired oven. His mezcal was clean and richly flavored, and I could detect similarities to Aurelio's spirit despite the obvious differences between father and son. Dad was tall and skinny, his hands gnarled and clothes worn, a large dagger on his hip. Son cut a fit figure in a clean, pressed, button-down blue shirt, shined cowboy boots, and a new-looking Stetson.

One of the other producers, Alfredo, pressed us to come for a drink at his home, a sweet little rancho surrounded by passion fruit, papaya, and pomegranate trees.

His wife proudly informed us that she grew them all organically. The two of them then plucked a few ripe fruits from the trees. Alfredo took out his pocketknife and started slicing fruit open for everyone. Our group had swelled to about a dozen by this point, village friends and palenqueros all sitting beneath the trees tearing into whole fruits like schoolchildren at snack time.

By the time we made it back to Aurelio's place, Sonia was anxiously awaiting us. She flitted about nervously, wanting everything to be perfect for our visit. All the men crushed into her tiny kitchen, crowding around the table. She served us Puebla's most famous

AURELIO GONZÁLEZ TOBÓN,
SAN PABLO AMEYALTEPEC.

dish, mole poblano: boiled chicken and rice smothered in a rich, dark sauce made from chiles and chocolate. (The chicken is inconsequential. This dish is all about the sauce.) Mole poblano is served only on the most celebratory of occasions. I was honored. I admitted to Sonia that I'd never had mole poblano before. It was delicious. She bowed her head gracefully. After the meal, Aurelio poured us the most special mezcal of all: pechuga.

In late fall through early winter, when tart mountain apples and plums are in season, certain mezcal makers in Oaxaca and Puebla prepare their most prized elixir. They start by collecting the rare mountain apples and plums. The still gets filled with 100 liters of finished mezcal and 100 kilos of the wild fruit, along with red plantain, pineapples, a handful of almonds, a few pounds of uncooked rice, and a whole chicken breast. The ingredients vary from village to village, producer to producer. The chicken breast—or it might be a turkey breast—gets washed under running water for about three hours, its skin removed but bone structure left intact, to get rid of all fat and grease. It's then suspended by strings in the air from the top of the still and a third distillation run begins. It's carried out slowly, lasting maybe twenty hours. The spirit's vapors pass over the breast (pechuga) as the fruit and meat flavors become infused in the liquid. When it's done, the breast has shrunk like jerky on the breast bone. It's removed from the still and hung in the family altar room, the most sacred space in the house.

Pechuga is a traditional and celebratory style of mezcal. But when I first came across it twenty years ago, it was not recognized under the official mezcal regulations. Pechuga was made illicitly for family and friends. There was no possibility of commercializing it, let alone exporting it. So, in 1996, after I'd been introduced to the style, I went to the Mezcal Regulatory Council to ask that they allow it. The first step was to submit a detailed application to the technical committee, but there were stacks of paperwork more to come. It would take three years to get pechuga certified. I even flew the country's top veterinarian out to Oaxaca to test the chickens' blood. (In addition to turkey, pechuga can also be made from wild rabbit or iguana. I have an old book on pulque from the 1950s that describes a mezcal made with goat meat.)

Del Maguey's first pechuga came from Santa Catarina Minas, made by Florencio Carlos Sarmiento and his son, Luis Carlos Vásquez. It's smoky and briny, with, indeed, the savoriness of chicken coming through. But the fruit shows well, too. When I've seen pechuga written about in the media, the meat gets all the attention—"There's a mezcal made with meat!"—that sort of thing. But the meat is not the point. It's the wild mountain apples, plums, plantains, and pineapples that are being celebrated. A chicken or turkey breast is used only to cut through the fruit's sweetness. The result is a sweet, savory spirit that drinks like a meal.

A few years back, I asked Don Lencho and Luis Carlos to make me a special version of pechuga. I'd become friendly with the chef José Andrés, who loves mezcal. The first time we drank together, he told me, "Hey, do you know what you should use to make your pechuga? You should use *pata negra!*" *Jamón Ibérico*, made from pure-bred, free-range, acorn-fed, black-footed Iberian pigs, is considered the best ham in the world. It's priced at well over a hundred dollars a pound. I laughed, "Yeah, right." But soon after, Andrés sent Chef Ruben García, who heads up his research and development team, to Oaxaca for a visit. A few months later, I received a strange package in Taos. It looked suspicious and I didn't recognize the sender, so I tried to get UPS to take it back. After some Googling, I realized the sender was Fermín, the finest Ibérico purveyor in Spain. Inside was a $2,000 bone-in haunch of cured ham. Staring at it, I knew I had two choices. Eat it or do what I knew José Andrés wanted me to do with it. I decided to do both. There was enough to go around. My partner, Sandra, and I started streaming YouTube videos on how to carve a *paleta* (shoulder) of jamón. I tasted a slice and it melted on the tongue like whipped butter. I took a dozen more slices, shrink-wrapped them, and hid them in a false bottom in my travel bag. On my next trip to Oaxaca, I delivered them to Don Lencho, who still makes our original pechuga, to make the first Pechuga Ibérico.

The results were delicious, but certainly nontraditional—spicy and floral, with deep, dark fruit notes and a lush, seductive body. I believe it's my responsibility at Del Maguey to preserve the liquid culture of Mexico. But I think I've earned the right to play with it some, too. Call it artistic license.

Until recently, Del Maguey carried only traditional pechuga and Ibérico. I felt no need to introduce another. That was until I went to Puebla. Aurelio's pechuga tastes of his wife's mole poblano—rich, spiced, meaty, and sweet. When I taste it now, the flavors put me right back in her cramped kitchen, surrounded by the hungry men of the village with a plate of steaming mole. I also think of the struggle to get mezcal from Puebla approved in the first place. It was a struggle that turned out to be futile, in the end, once the law was revised. Yet I can't help wonder how many other great mezcals are out there, in places not yet approved by the powers that be. Only nine states are officially recognized as mezcal-producing regions. Families in more than a dozen other states make mezcal that is unsanctioned. There must be gems among them.

THE PATRIARCH OF SAN PABLO
AMEYALTEPEC, AURELIO'S FATHER,
JOSÉ LUIS.

LIGHTING THE TRUNK WOOD IN THE
HORNO, SAN PABLO AMEYALTEPC.

DEL MAGUEY PUEBLA

VINO DE MEZCAL

Despite having one of the oldest distilling traditions in the country, Puebla just joined NOM 70 in 2016. Our mezcal from Puebla hails from a semitropical valley in the shadow of two volcanoes. The plants are harvested at ten to fifteen years of age, roasted in underground earthen ovens, fermented in the open air, and distilled to proof a single time. Thanks to a hybrid alembic-column still known as a *resaque* (reflux) still, full distillation is achieved with a single run. The vapors pass through a column containing three copper plates, each of which condenses the vapor separately, increasing its purity as it rises. The result is an incredibly floral spirit, carnation and lilac against a backdrop of ripe tropical fruit and a hint of spice. It's crisp yet creamy, as round and soft in the mouth as fresh *queso de cabra* (goat cheese), and finishes with delightful finesse, remarkable complexity, and memorable minerality.

Production Notes

VILLAGE: San Pablo Ameyaltepec

PALENQUERO: Aurelio González Tobón

STATE: Puebla

REGION: Mixteca Poblana

MAGUEY: Papalote, Pizorra (*Agave potatorum, A. marmorata*)

AGE OF MAGUEY: 12–18 years

ELEVATION: 5,216 feet (1,590 meters)

ROAST DURATION: 3–5 days

TYPE OF WOOD: Oak

SIZE OF TINAS: 200 L

FERMENTATION DURATION: 6–9 days

WATER SOURCE: Spring

STILL TYPE: Copper/reflux 3 plates

STILL SIZE: 80 L

ABV OF MEZCAL: 47%

VOL MEZCAL PRODUCED PER TINA: 12–15 L

CHAPTER 10

THE THEFT

The greatest comedian in the world was from Mexico. Mario Fortino Alfonso Moreno Reyes, who went by the stage name Cantinflas, appeared in more than fifty films during the last century and is known as Mexico's answer to Charlie Chaplin. But Chaplin knew better. He proclaimed Cantinflas the best comedian alive. He had a sweet, goofy smile, eyes set wide apart, and a Fu Manchu mustache. A hat worn too small for his head had audiences giggling before he even said a word. He was known for a fast-talking, roundabout way of speaking. His persona was all about making fun of the moneyed, the establishment. His most famous lines became popular expressions in Mexico. He would say, "*Usted no se despreocupe*"—"Don't un-worry yourself." And my favorite: "*Ni modo chato!*"—"No worries, dude!"

I use that one a lot. Ni modo chato.

One morning not long ago, I awoke in Oaxaca to some disturbing news. (My bed is still in the bodega, a plain double mattress in the corner of the unheated top floor amid cases and tanks of mezcal. It gets so cold at night that I used to sleep up there with a tarp over my blankets. For years, I had no windows to keep the frigid air out. I would wake up in the middle of the night and see a white owl perched on the rafter above me. Just staring down. I finally got sick of the cold and the birds waking me each morning with their loud squawking, so I installed windows—but no curtains. It's like sleeping in an aquarium. The fields outside my window and the mountain in the distance are the panoramic masterpiece I wake up to each morning.) The news I got that day was about work. A shipment of mezcal bound for the US that left Teotitlán del Valle a few days prior had been hijacked in Puebla, not too far from Nochixtlán. The driver said he'd been held at gunpoint as two men unloaded all twenty-four pallets from the truck and transferred them to their own. Tens of thousands of dollars' worth of mezcal gone. Del Maguey is insured, but to think of the labor that went into producing all that mezcal stung. Then the realization that the mezcal was probably headed for the black market hit. I've heard of fences in the area who send stolen goods straight to the western coast of Mexico, where ships bound for China await.

I'd been robbed before. As a young man, I once had all my art supplies and humble possessions stolen from a storage container while I was traveling in Europe. Years later, my good friend Pancho was found to have embezzled from Del Maguey after being corrupted by an engineer in the city. The pain of that betrayal cut deep, and I've never fully recovered from it. But this was the first time Del Maguey was targeted. The hardest part of the ordeal was telling the guys who work with me at the bodega in Teotitlán. These are the men charged with rinsing the bottles in mezcal (we use the tails of distillation) before bottling and packaging them, and assisting Arturo

KISSING THE CROSS BEFORE BLESSING THE ROAST.

in the office as needed. They stood around, hands to open mouths, eyes wide, shaking their heads. They felt violated. They were angry. (Pancho's brother, Mito, still works with us and was visibly unsettled, mumbling to himself in disbelief.) Me, not so much. *Ni modo chato.* I had heard over the years of tequila shipments being hijacked, but I hadn't expected it. In retrospect, I should have. I now see that it was inevitable. Mezcal, the spirit no one wanted just a decade ago, is now coveted. And Del Maguey is a visible target. We've since made arrangements to beef up security for shipments. And I should probably make my own security a priority, too.

It just so happened that Carlos Camarena, the prolific tequila producer, came to visit me the very same day we learned of the theft. Known for producing El Tesoro, Tapatio, and Ocho, three of the most esteemed brands, he's well respected for resisting industry pressure to sacrifice integrity in favor of the bottom line. He was on vacation with his family in Oaxaca and surprised me at the bodega, materializing at my door with a wide smile and open arms. I shared with him privately what had happened. He understood better than anyone, as he has lived through kidnapping and extortion attempts. In the highlands of Jalisco, where his distillery is located, high-profile tequila producers are targeted by thugs for ransoms. Carlos has taken precautions to protect himself and his family, taking a different vehicle to work every day so he won't be easily recognized. But his town is too small for him to remain completely anonymous.

I wanted to cheer up my team and put on a brave face for Carlos that day. "Want to go on an adventure?" I asked him. "Sure!" He responded. He, his daughter, and a couple guys from the bodega piled into two pickups and we set out. Our destination was yet another mountain village, a trip like I'd made many times. But I knew it would be life-changing for Carlos. The adventures I take people on in Oaxaca always are. Coming from Jalisco and the tequila industry, Carlos, I knew, was in for a culture shock. His distillery is small and his production methods artisanal, but compared to the primitive palenques of Oaxaca, his facility is highly sophisticated. Most impressive, I suspected, would be the breadth of maguey varieties. In tequila country, only blue agave is permitted. In Oaxaca, diversity abounds. (The thing is, wild agave used to abound in Jalisco as well, but the tequila industry quashed that diversity in the late nineteenth century when it chose to use only blue agave—another misguided effort to regulate the ancient craft of mezcal. Tequila, after all, was once known as *vino de mezcal de la región de Tequila*: mezcal wine from the Tequila region.)

Mezcal is changing, turning into a global industry. Del Maguey has changed, too. I started it as an art project and an adventure. We are now a global brand. We've managed to scale up production organically, without altering the process. In certain villages, we added hornos, molinos, tinas, stills. But the palenques are still rustic open-air structures. One or two have installed electric lights to facilitate working at night. We've encouraged our more ambitious palenqueros to streamline their work cycle, starting a new roast while the last one is fermenting, rather than completing an entire production run from beginning to end before starting again. I'm skeptical of claims made by industry experts that mezcal is at risk of losing its soul, that it could become as industrialized as tequila. After more than two decades in Oaxaca, I've seen the villages we work with progress. But the integrity of the mezcal hasn't been touched. The spirit is as pure and awe-inspiring as it ever was.

I do, however, feel increased pressure to act as a guardian of mezcal. I see that the spirit is sought after. And I'm aware that other companies entering the market might not prioritize preserving the culture of mezcal. It's my hope and belief that, as Del Maguey continues to expand its reach, we will serve as an example of how to grow sustainably. The rusticity of mezcal is part of its romance, but the reality of it reflects rampant poverty within the state of Oaxaca. The mezcal industry can be a force for boosting economic development in rural communities there. It can change people's lives for the better, if it's done right. I remember a time when the families I worked with all slept huddled in one room on the dirt floor. Working with Del Maguey has provided them with indoor plumbing, access to the Internet, better health care, and opportunities for a better education for their children. We must be doing something right: in twenty-three years and counting, not a single palenquero has left the Del Maguey family.

Out on the road, with the tequila maker Carlos Camarena, I watched his face light up when he saw wild maguey growing right out of the rock face as we drove up into the hills. He asked if we could stop to pick a baby plant or two. He keeps a collection of different agave species in his garden back home. I chuckled to myself as he scrambled a few steps up the rocky mountain to pluck a maguey pup. He was on vacation in his own country, but a foreigner out here all the same.

"Did you get a good one?"

"Oh yes," he beamed proudly, showing off his plantlet.

He settled back, buckled in, and we sped off toward the next great adventure.

CHAPTER 11

THE CORNFIELDS

BUENA VISTA LAS MILPAS.

As they age, some people get sick. Others lose their eyesight or become arthritic. Me, I'm losing my fingerprints.

I am baffled. I've rubbed various creams on my fingertips in the hopes of preserving the fine grooves mapped out on them. But no matter what I do, my fingerprints keep fading. They're as smooth as eggshells. The scanners at the airport barely register my prints and I almost always end up with a big X on my printout at Global Entry. I sometimes worry about what would happen if I got arrested. If you can't take someone's fingerprints, how do you identify them? *Ni modo chato*. I like the idea of treading lightly, leaving nothing behind. I've learned to practice letting go. That way, everything becomes a gift.

Like San Pedro Taviche.

My friend Jorge Quiroz was a journalist for the daily newspaper in Oaxaca. We met when he started writing a column on mezcal. We'd get together to talk and taste. Eventually, he published a slender book on the spirit. One day, he told me about a remote village called San Pedro Taviche that made beautiful mezcal. He'd heard about it through a banker friend of his whose office was directly in front of the Central de Abastos market in downtown Oaxaca. The banker had met some of the village elders from San Pedro Taviche when they were in the city to fill out some official paperwork for a grant. The village kept getting bypassed for infrastructure improvements, like electrification, medical clinics, new roads, new schools. The elders were illiterate and unable to complete the required applications for government funds. The banker offered to help. They paid him in mezcal.

Jorge, his banker friend, and I set out for San Pedro Taviche together during Día de los Muertos. We were accompanied by my younger daughter, Sadie Ray, who was visiting, a writer-photographer duo from the UK, and a team of videographers from Mexico City shooting a short film called *Fuego Verde*. We took two vehicles. San Pedro Taviche is located in the most remote corner of the Ocotlán district, in the deep south of Oaxaca's Valles Centrales. From Teotitlán, you have to go over three mountains to get there. The road was rocky and as dry as the desert. There were a few little springs along the way and the odd rancho here and there, but little else. Suddenly, the road dropped down into a tropical valley. When it came to a T, we could have sworn we were deep in the jungle. A guy walked around the corner, the first person we'd seen in miles, and he was dressed in the most peculiar outfit. He wore a green felt sombrero with brightly colored peacock feathers sticking arched around the brim. He stared at us like we were from outer space. We hung a left, drove into the village, and came face-to-face with about fifty Indians. They all wore green felt sombreros with peacock feathers in them, Levis rolled up to their knees, and huaraches. They were playing volleyball.

It was nearly dusk as we rolled into this pueblito. From amid the group of men at play stepped the *presidente municipal*, who extended his hand to greet us. After initial introductions, he led us out of the village center to a large hill covered with cornfields. On top were four small single-room houses surrounding a patch of dirt forming a tiny plaza in the center. There we met Alberto Hernández Luis, aka Don Beto, the man we had come to find. Don Beto had a round face and balding head and wore a wide, warm smile. We followed him into a ravine for about half a kilometer until we came to his palenque, a humble log-and-tin structure surrounded by banana trees. The still produced only 150 liters at a time. Don Beto made his mezcal from the wild magueys that grew in the hills nearby. He harvested wild espadín, tobalá, tepextate—whatever was ripest and closest to him. Because the palenque was on a hill, it made use of gravity. The roasted piñas were rolled from the horno, one at a time, down to a big black rock where two guys mashed it by hand with what looked like giant croquet mallets.

After our tour of the palenque, we headed back to Don Beto's house. By this time, it was dark. No street lights. We could barely see the ground beneath our feet. Don Beto stored his mezcal in one of the four houses on the main square. His mother—I guessed he was a bachelor—was at the doorway holding back a barking dog by the scruff of its neck. Don Beto beckoned us into another house, where I spotted the wildest altar I've ever seen: just a couple of candles burning on the floor in the corner and a four-foot-high mass of orange wildflowers from the mountains. He poured us a taste of his mezcal out of a Coke bottle. It was unbelievable.

As we were talking and sipping out of the little clay cups I'd distributed to everyone, my eyes drifted past our host to the walls of his little house. The entire thing was built out of giant maguey flower stalks. Quiotes. They were planted in the earth, these thick, dried stems. And where the wall met the roof, there was a row of *cántaros*, black clay jugs used for storing mezcal, lining the house all the way around. I'd never seen anything like it. Snapping out of it, I asked what I could buy from him and we settled on twenty-five liters. I would drink it myself and share it with friends.

"Can I buy some more?" I inquired after a while. "How much can you make for me? I'll buy it every year."

"I can make a thousand liters a year."

"Great! Let's make a deal," I said. "When can I come back for more?"

But it wasn't going to be that easy. Don Beto said, "Wait a minute. Easy does it." And I knew I wasn't going to like what came next. "I can't sell to you unless you buy from the other two producers in this village."

"Oh. But I never tasted their mezcal. I like your mezcal," I told him.

"I know," he said. "But if you don't buy from them, I'll get the *mal de ojo*—the evil eye—and I'll die."

What can you say to that? I thanked him and told him I loved his mezcal, but that I'd have to think about his proposal.

Over the next couple of years, I shared and drank twenty-five liters of San Pedro Taviche. Three or four years later, I went back and Don Beto was happy to see me. I bought more mezcal from him to take home, but not enough to bottle. In nine years, I went back to visit with Don Beto four more times. Sometimes, I took guests with me. Each time, I held out hope that I might finally get him to sell me enough mezcal to bottle for Del Maguey. Each time, he reiterated his terms.

A few years ago, I went with Cosme, Pancho's father. Don Beto invited us into his home where he pulled out an emerald green five-gallon jug of mezcal. He poured it into smaller plastic water bottles and served us from those. We sat and sipped out of little clay cups as he shared with us that this was his last mezcal.

"It's over," he said. "My knees are gone. I can't go up into the forest anymore to harvest the wild espadín, the wild tobalá, and the wild tepextate. I can't even walk up through the arroyo to my palenque."

I was crushed.

"Don Beto, thank you so much," I told him. "You've been so wonderful. If I can ever help you, just tell me." And then it occurred to me that I could help this sweet man. I told him he could get an operation on his knees. I offered to pay for it. He could trade me mezcal in return. He never gave me an answer.

Instead, he said, "My brother always wanted to buy my palenque, but it was my profession. How could I sell him my palenque? But now that I can't walk up there anymore . . . Here. Let's have another." He filled the water bottle anew and we drank that, too. Between sips, we paid our respects to the Virgin of Juquila, whose picture hung above his wild altar.

"I don't have any more mezcal," Don Beto announced after we'd finished the jug. "But my brother has a store in front of the church in the village. He has all that's left over. You can buy it from him. And the good news is that his son is coming back from Chicago where he works in the night vegetable market. I'll sell them my palenque, and they can install it down in the cornfield right below my house. It will have the same water source, a healthy spring that runs through here. My brother and his son will do the bulk of the work, and I will still go down at the very end and do the final adjustments."

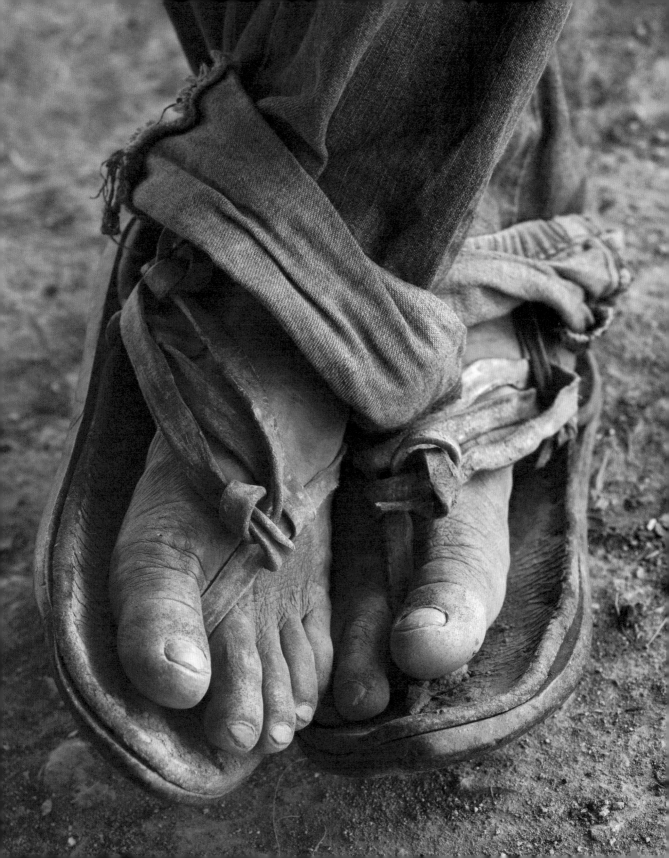

It sounded promising. We said our good-byes and I went in search of his brother's store. There I met Don Beto's brother, Don Roberto, who sold me five liters. I told him I'd be back.

Once the palenque was moved closer to Don Beto's house, I returned. Don Roberto and his son welcomed me with eggs, beans, homemade tortillas, and their first batch of mezcal. It was just as good as when Don Beto made it alone. I bought sixty liters from them and made a deal to buy more each year. (Don Roberto must have been a less superstitious man than his brother. He didn't seem to worry about neighbors giving him the evil eye.) I had labels made for San Pedro Taviche, anticipating selling it as part of Del Maguey's Vino de Mezcal series. Because the maguey varieties changed for each batch, I made sure it read, "Taviche gets its unique changing flavor from the blending of various wild agaves: 100% pure unpropagated espadín, tobalá, tobasiche or tepextate." It was all finally happening and I was thrilled. But the next year, when I visited, Don Roberto and his son had only fifteen liters to sell me. The year after that, they had none because they drank it all at the annual village fiesta. The following year, it was twenty-five liters. I was losing hope that I could continue to buy from them.

After a few more months, I finally had to give up. It was too much trouble to travel all the way out to Taviche for such small quantities. Time to start mourning the end of my supply—I had just twenty-five liters left. Just as I was mentally rationing the last of it, I got a call from Arturo.

"Hey, they've got a hundred liters," he said. "Should I buy it?"

"Hell, yes!"

A month or so later, he called again. "They've got seventy liters more. But they say that's it for the year. Should I buy what they have?"

"Fuck, yeah."

Before I came along, Don Beto eked out a living selling his mezcal to friends and neighbors. You might expect someone in his position to jump at the chance to sell to an outsider who wants a steady supply. But his reluctance to work with me was not uncommon. Many of the Zapotec (or Mixe or Mixteca) farmers I've met are content living the way they've always lived. The younger generation tends to harbor ambitions to expand the family business. But the old guard is unhurried. They think, *Why would we want more? We have everything we need.* And who am I to argue with that? I'm a guest in their country, an inductee into their culture. My desire to share their craft can't supersede my duty to preserve their traditions. So, when I approach a new village about joining Del Maguey, I am unhurried, too. I wait and see. Sometimes it takes a decade to finally cement the relationship. And sometimes I have to let go of a mezcal I love. Set it free. If I'm lucky, it will come back to me.

DEL MAGUEY
SAN PEDRO TAVICHE

VINO DE MEZCAL

Made in a remote mountain valley corner of Ocotlán, this mezcal took nine long years to make itself available to us. Taviche gets its unique flavor from the blending of three wild agaves: espadín, tobalá, and tepextate. The pit-roasted hearts are ground by two men using giant mallets, fermented naturally by airborne microbes, and distilled twice in a copper still. The mezcal shows layers of dried fruit—dates and raisins—as well as hazelnuts, sweet cedar, and a hint of chocolate. Notes of dried tarragon and nutmeg linger in the background.

Production Notes

VILLAGE: San Pedro Taviche

PALENQUEROS: Alberto "Don Beto" Hernandez Luis, Juan Hernández, and Laurentino Hernández

STATE: Oaxaca

REGION: Valles Centrales

MAGUEY: Espadín, tobalá, tepextate (*Agave angustifolia* Haw., *A. potatorum*, *A. marmorata*)

AGE OF MAGUEY: 30 years

ELEVATION: 5,250 feet (1,600 meters)

STILL SIZE: 350 L

STILL TYPE: Copper

STILL SIZE: 180 L

ABV OF MEZCAL: 49%

But it's not always this way. There are times mezcal finds me even when my eyes are closed, when my mind is elsewhere. When it's the last thing I'm looking for.

One year, as a sophomore living in Ojai, California, I took an after-school job with a man named Buck Dollarhide. Buck was a Navajo Indian and the foreman of a project for a new water storage tank. He paid me fifteen dollars an hour in cash, really good money for a teenager to make back then. The project involved sandblasting the interior of the tank before it could be coated with a waterproof epoxy. My job was to head a crew of teenagers shoveling the spent sand out through a one-yard opening. I breathed in dust for months. Later, I would take up smoking. But I'm pretty sure it was that summer job that kicked the shit out of my lungs. Now, when I visit palenques, I struggle up the hills to see the maguey fields. I run out of breath easily and need to pause to catch it before carrying on. The palenqueros are patient with me.

Otherwise, I'm in good health. When I'm not in Oaxaca, I'm at home in Taos, making art. Or I'm on the road promoting Del Maguey. Or I'm racing cars, my old hobby having taken over my life again. A couple years back, when Del Maguey started achieving the sort of success I'd never dreamed possible, I once more found myself with some fuck-you money. This time, I would use it to indulge my first love: speed. I bought myself a 1929 Model A Ford chassis and a 1931 engine and built myself a vehicle: 1922 Roadster cab, 1927 Model T turtle deck, five-speed transmission, rack and pinion steering, downdraft Stromberg carburetor, electronic ignition, racing camshaft and headers. I drove it in The Race of Gentlemen, an annual hot-rod competition held on a strip of beach in New Jersey. A car has to have an engine from 1953 or earlier to enter, and the car body must date to 1934 or earlier. My first day out, I won eight out of ten races. It gave me the kind of thrill I felt years ago, drag racing illegally in Ojai at night. I love the sense of freedom you get on the open road. There's a rebelliousness involved in building a machine whose sole purpose is to achieve speed. I still want to feel that, to be the bad boy I was at nineteen.

I drive across the US at least once a year, usually to get my hot rod to a race on one coast or the other. And I continue to clock in thousands of miles in Oaxaca. Cars were a big part of my journey into mezcal. It takes a love of driving, after all, to want to spend hours cruising up and down mountain roads in search of maguey and molinos. These days, I'm not actively looking for new mezcals to add to Del Maguey's collection, but they still manage to find me.

In the early days, I'd sometimes have Indians showing up at my door after hearing I had good mezcal, looking for a taste. They were always suspicious when they saw me. How could a gringo know what real mezcal is? I'd pour a little out and— *saca palabras!* It "grabbed the words," meaning that it caused them to start rapping.

These days, the tables have turned. They sometimes show up on my doorstep to offer me a taste of their own mezcal. They've heard about Del Maguey and want to work with me. It means I've tasted a good deal of bad mezcal. But I've also been pleasantly surprised.

One Sunday afternoon not too long ago, on my way back from a trip to the market in Tlacolula, I was about to steer my Jeep up the road to the bodega when I spotted my neighbor and compadre, Don Gaspar, through the arch of his open door. Don Gaspar grew up as a humble goatherd and later became a weaver. He was a dedicated supporter of his children and sent his son, Demetrio, to good schools. Demetrio took up weaving, as well, and soon became a master craftsman. He now exhibits his work around the country and beyond. From their large, airy work space, Demetrio creates beautiful tapestries and teaches classes on organic wool dyeing and loom weaving. His works are displayed in a corner of the inside courtyard where tourists can browse and buy. He also runs a bed and breakfast out of the building called La Cúpula, where my guests usually stay. Demetrio's wife, Maribel, makes wholesome Zapotec breakfasts that fortify them for the day.

I hadn't seen Don Gaspar for some time and decided to pop in to say hello. I found him sitting in the courtyard with a friend of his, an elderly man who had one eye squeezed halfway shut into a slit. An old injury, I guessed. The man wore a broad rolled-brim tan felt sombrero. A beautiful hat, classic in style. On his feet he had homemade huaraches, in the ancient style you find in the codices. Gaspar introduced us.

"This is my friend, Anastasio," he said. "He makes mezcal." My knee-jerk reaction when I hear this is, "Yeah, right." I've heard it before. People are always trying to get me to taste their mezcal or their friend's mezcal. If I'm not in the mood, I politely decline. That day, I wasn't in the mood.

"I just came to say hello to you, Gaspar," I said. But as anyone who has visited the shop can attest, he can be a persistent old dude. He urged me to try it. I relented and, in a rare moment without a copita, went down into the kitchen for a couple of clean glasses. Anastasio carefully poured me a taste of his spirit. As it filled my mouth, my eyes went round. It was a jaw dropper. We got to talking in that old, genteel Spanish I speak with the Zapotecs. It's an abbreviated Spanish, short and simple instead of full of flowers.

"Where do you make this?" I asked him.

"I make it in Las Milpas." The Cornfields.

"And where is that?"

"Over by San Dionisio." I know the place. I pass it on the way to Chichicapa and Minas.

"I'm really poor," he continued. "My three sons and I, we don't have a car. We have to rent somebody else's palenque."

"Well, my first producer, his name is Faustino. As a matter of fact, he also had to rent a still when I first met him. When we started working together, I bought him a still of his own."

At this, Anastasio popped his eyes.

"Don *R-r-r-on*?" he gasped, rolling his R dramatically. It turned out that he and Faustino were friends. I asked if I could buy a liter or two from him. Don Gaspar shook his head.

"I come to Teotitlán from my village every Sunday with a five-liter jug. I can't sell just one liter," he explained. "No. You have to buy all of it."

I agreed and told him to meet me at our bodega next door to make the transaction. A little while later, I heard a knock. It was Anastasio, and he sounded distraught. I opened the door to find a swarm of bees attacking him. He was swatting at them, yelping, flailing. I ushered him in, let him catch his breath before asking if I could take a short video of him. Just a brief portrait, a little record I like to keep of my first meetings with producers. "What's your name? Where do you come from?" That sort of thing. In the video, he dutifully replies, sweet man.

"I like your flavor," I said to him, a common way of expressing admiration for someone's mezcal. "I'd like to keep tasting it. If I remember the flavor of it, I'm going to have to start buying from you."

He gave me a relative's phone number. I told him we'd be in touch. But time moves slowly here. People aren't in a rush. A full year went by before I decided to make the trip to Las Milpas. I had some good friends from Kyoto and the king of barbecue Steven Raichlen visiting, and I knew I'd be driving by San Dionisio. We'll stop in Milpas, I thought. I dug up the number Anastasio had given me and, miraculously, he answered. We made a plan to meet in the market.

By the time our little group made it to San Dionisio, it was late morning. I had no trouble finding Anastasio. It turned out it had been his eldest son's wedding the night before, and the party was still winding down. The family was gathered not in a house but in a makeshift shelter made of carrizo and covered with a tarp. The women were washing the big mole pots and dishes. The uncles were all leaning against the wall, hungover and bleary-eyed as they recuperated from the all-nighter they'd pulled. They dragged over a table from somewhere and we all sat down together. Anastasio poured us some mezcal. His eldest son Rigoberto and my friends all shared a toast. The mezcal was incredible. Anastasio said he made it sometime before 2000, a batch big enough for all three sons' weddings. We noted the depth and mellowness of it. *Añejado en vidrio*: aged in glass.

"It's so good to meet you all," I said after an hour or so. "Now, can we go to Las Milpas?"

"Oh, no," Anastasio told me. "It's too late and we live far up in the hills. Another time."

Only then did he reveal that it was another several hours-long climb over the mountain to get to Las Milpas by car. Anastasio and his family thought nothing of making the trip on foot: three hours in each direction, along steep, winding, rocky mountainside roads. We decided to save the visit for a later date.

It wasn't until the following year that I finally made it out to Las Milpas. I headed out with Arturo in the Jeep, and we stopped in San Dionisio to pick up Anastasio's nephew, Roberto, the village's assistant mayor. He directed us out of town and up this dirt road until we came to an arroyo. It was the last residential part of San Dionisio, nothing but barren mountain beyond. Here we picked up Roberto's wife, who was in high heels and a chic dress. It was a special occasion, her riding up with us to see her relatives. A vehicle is a luxury. The Jeep climbed the mountain in four-wheel drive, barely making it up the craggier stretches. Once we got to Las Milpas, I saw that it wasn't a village at all, but a rancho—just a handful of ramshackle houses at the top of these rolling hills. In the far distance, I could see the maguey fields they'd planted and goats roaming. It was like a frame from the Sergei Eisenstein film, *¡Que viva México!*, about early Mexican life.

In this idyllic setting, I met Anastasio's family. One brother no longer drank mezcal. He'd drunk so much, he drank himself out of drinking. But he smoked. The three sons were all there with their women. The women all wore bandanas; one of them had a new baby gently swaying in a hammock in the rickety carrizo cook house. They each greeted me by bowing low, a sign of respect, then taking my hands in theirs and kissing them. These mountain people had fascinating customs. The family kept dogs that hunted *tejón*: badgers. Now, most people don't know what a badger looks like. Picture a wolverine. You might not know what a wolverine is either, but just by the sound of it you know it's bad. The dogs' faces were covered in scratches and old scars from the badgers' claws. The dogs hunted at night, broke the badgers' necks, then carried them home in their maws. Anastasio's family skinned and ate them, tossing the dogs the bones. This here was Oaxacan hillbilly country.

Anastasio brought out three mezcals: the wedding mezcal I'd tasted a year before, an espadín, and one he called *mezcal del campo*. Mezcal of the field. It's a blend that changes with each batch depending on what magueys are ripest and closest to the palenque. I took one taste and immediately told Anastasio that I'd build him a palenque if he wanted one.

"How are we going to pay you?" he asked.

"Just keep making great mezcal," I told him. We agreed, and then all the men headed out on foot to visit the maguey fields. It was way down one mountain and up another. And me with my compromised lungs, I almost died. But we came up over the last hill and it was just like heaven. A vision of rolling green hills dotted with live-stock, maguey sprouting from the rugged terrain. It was beautiful.

I returned to Las Milpas when the palenque was completed. The family was holding a proper inauguration with a feast. I promised to bring fireworks, bottle rockets with the long bamboo tail. Arturo, Jimmy Yeager of Jimmy's in Aspen, his son Luca, and Steve Olson all came along. Anastasio offered me *las quinientos gotas*, the first five hundred drops out of the still. It wasn't rectified—Anastasio hadn't yet blended heads, heart, and tails—and the still was brand-new, so it hadn't yet been properly seasoned, but the mezcal was still amazing. To celebrate our new relation-ship, the women poured out big bowls of *tejate*, a sweet, milky drink made from ground maize and cacao.

"We drink this only at important celebrations," they explained. Even the bowls were remarkable, gourds hand-painted in bright colors with flowers and scenes of wildlife, ducks floating in a lake. They served a simple soup of green beans in a delicate clear broth. There were tortillas for dipping and maybe the most flavorful picante salsa I've had in any village. I was struck again, like I was so often in the beginning, by how little these people had yet how hospitable they could be. They made a feast out of a few meager preparations.

Mezcal del Campo has become a part of the Del Maguey line. I acknowledge that, when I started this venture, I was naive. I was so impressed by all the different maguey varieties that I made them a focus of the craft. Now, I see newcomers to the spirit who are already obsessed with one variety or another. It has put undue pressure on certain wild maguey populations. Field blends like the one Anastasio makes are the true roots of mezcal. The first makers didn't care about varietals, didn't glorify one plant over another. They cared only about making great mezcal. Picking what's ripest and nearest the palenque is a sustainability measure in itself, a practical and sensible approach to production, and results in deliciously complex mezcal.

RIGOBERTO, ELDEST SON OF ANASTASIO.

ROBERTO, ANASTASIO'S BROTHER, WITH A
TEJÓN (BADGER) TAIL ON HIS SOMBREORO.

BOCA DEL CERRO

From the very first, I knew I wanted to plant maguey. Such spectacular plants, my green thumb was itching. In the market in Tlacolula, I found some espadín pups and planted them in my backyard in Teotitlán. When I moved to the bodega, I transplanted the maguey. Those plants gave hijuelos. I would spend my mornings with a razor blade slicing the bulbs in half to propagate baby plants. (You climb a ladder and cut the bulbils at the top of the quiote, just as they're about to burst. The leftover stub sprout shoots high up in the air. Maguey flowers, food of the ancients, can be boiled and mixed into scrambled eggs or used in escabeche. I experimented with eating them different ways during this time.) In time, my collection grew to about six thousand baby magueys. They were "loaned" to San Luis del Río and planted above the palenque. I was proud of them, like a papa. But the itch was still there. I started to think, *I want to plant my own field.*

Andrés Hernández had been my assistant at the bodega in Teotitlán. He's a weaver, lives up the hill from the bodega. He's also an excellent water witch. (He'll cut a supple, Y-shaped branch from a tree and use it to dowse for water. I learned from him how to do this and found water for a new well in Chichicapa.) Andrés ran the bottling line, kept the bodega clean, was great at tending to our little garden. I knew he had some land, a rare stretch at the foot of a mountain that was carved with ancient terraces. Terracing is an age-old practice designed to prevent rainfall runoff on steep slopes. These vast steps had been etched into the mountain by hand a millennium ago. A small ravine runs through them, providing hydration. The first time I saw it, I was in awe. I remember feeling the antiquity of the place. It was precivilized. *Ru'udain,* they call it in Zapotec, meaning Boca del Cerro—the mouth of the mountain. It would be perfect for planting maguey.

Andrés wasn't a farmer and hadn't planted anything on his land in years. I asked if I could rent it from him. We struck a classic deal called *medias,* where the landowner puts up the land and is responsible for keeping it weed-free, while the tenant provides the plants. When all is said and done, the two parties split the yield fifty-fifty.

In 2007, I planted fifteen hundred two-year-old maguey pups. I'd paid some men with tractors to clear the land, which was overgrown with thorn trees. But I did much of the knees-in-the-dirt labor myself, backbreaking work. A couple guys helped me turn the soil and fashion the rows and *surcos,* the furrows between rows. I'd heard the best strategy was to plant two meters apart for every row and three meters apart for each surco, a sparse and open planting to give the magueys plenty of room to grow into. We would start work early, toil all morning, and then take a break before noon for lunch. One day, as we sat in the shade of a thorn tree and shared tlayudas, beans, and chiles, a goatherd passing by stopped to join us. It was like we'd all gathered for a picnic in the country.

SCENES FROM OUR TWENTIETH ANNIVERSARY PARTY.

Andrés was meant to clear the field of weeds twice each year. The first year, he took advantage of all the space between the rows and planted black beans there, a common practice among maguey farmers. You typically have five years to grow corn, beans, and squash between the rows before the plants grow too big to get a team of oxen through them. The piggybacking crops also help keep weeds at bay. Certain crops, like beans, reintroduce nitrogen into the soil, keeping it healthy. Andrés got a great bean harvest that year. The following year, I went to check on how the plants were doing. They hadn't been weeded all year.

"Andrés, what happened?!" I asked. "*Es qué . . . pero, pero . . .*" he stuttered. Excuses. I was disappointed. His father asked if we could work out a similar deal in his own field, which was adjacent to the field that belonged to Andrés. I figured I'd double down on my investment. Now, I had three thousand maguey growing at the mouth of the mountain. I returned periodically to check on the fields, but it became clear that neither was ever weeded. After nine years, I considered it a loss. In twenty years in Oaxaca, it was only the second time an oral contract wasn't kept.

In the seventh year, I took Paciano, from San Luis del Río, up to see my plants. They were tiny and spindly and he immediately dismissed them as worthless, calling me out for my foolishness. I was embarrassed. It hadn't been a huge financial investment, but the time and energy I'd spent felt like a waste. The next year, terrible rains washed out the roads and it was impossible to get up to the terraces. The following year, I took Faustino up to get his opinion.

"*Maduro*," he told me. "These are ripe." An experienced farmer, he could tell the plants were ready to harvest. The wilt of the leaves, the color of them, told him the plants had absorbed all the nutrients they could and had reached the peak of maturity. If we didn't harvest them soon, they'd start to decay. I was shocked, then giddy. Most of the hearts weren't very big. These were choked, stressed, suffering maguey. But, as Faustino said to me, maguey are like people: some are bigger, some are smaller. Some mature faster, some slower. He asked if he could take the harvested piñas back to Chichicapa to make mezcal.

We began the harvest at the corner of the field. I decided to take every other plant. I didn't take the best ones or the ripest. I just went, "Take this one and leave the next," row after row, for the entire field. The rest were left for Andrés, per our deal, even though he hadn't held up his end of it. Faustino and his son, Maximino, carried out the harvest. They cut down the plants using machetes, which they wielded with practiced skill. By the end of it, we had harvested fifteen hundred plants. It came out to four and a half tons. Usually, a ten-ton roast is made up of about 150 piñas. The hearts from Boca del Cerro were dwarfs.

As we were harvesting, Andrés mentioned that he would be willing to sell me the rest of the yield. What would he do with fifteen hundred maguey? I agreed and got another five tons out of it. A total of three thousand plants weighing in at less than ten tons. Once Faustino finished the mezcal and we tasted it, however, we were blown away. It was Chichicapa—everything he makes is. You can't change the hand of the maker. But it had layers and depth beyond anything Faustino had ever made. The plants had suffered. They'd changed. They struggled to gain mass, shooting their roots down deep into the earth in search of nutrients. This was espadín, but it tasted like something else. It had the deeply concentrated mineral character of tobalá. I thought of all the winemakers I'd heard in Europe talking about how the vines needed to be stressed, they had to suffer to produce great wine. Maguey suffers. It absorbs cosmic energy, and gives back to us. It's such a generous plant. I hold my arms up like the leaves of the maguey and turn my face to the sky. All I can do is accept the plant's gift.

Boca del Cerro is Del Maguey's twentieth anniversary mezcal. It's fitting that Faustino, my first collaborator, should make it. It's like coming full circle. We threw a huge party in Oaxaca to mark the occasion. It felt good to finally host all our producers who had invited me to eat and drink at innumerable fiestas. The party was held at a friend's restaurant, the food and drink were unlimited. A jazz band and an eighteen-piece village brass band played. We provided transport and hotel rooms for all. Our producers, some close Oaxacan friends, and several of the bartenders who have supported Del Maguey all came. Steve Olson oversaw the cocktails. Michael Gardner was making the rounds, still glowing from having recently published his first collection of poems. Mezcal makers from remote villages a day's travel apart came together for the first time. Alejandra danced with Rogelio, Paciano drank with Espiridión. People who never would have met realized they were part of the same family.

I'll never plant Boca del Cerro again. The ruggedness of the land and lack of attention from the landowner were too much to endure again. Consequently, this mezcal will never be made again. Tasting it is like experiencing a fleeting piece of art—a concert, a dance performance, the Buddhist sand mandalas of Tibet. A banging party. When it's over, only the memory of it remains.

At another great party in another part of the world, I floated through the crowd on a similar high, my toes barely touching the ground. It was the Venice Biennale, in 2011, a massive exhibition of LA artists called Venice in Venice. I agreed to participate if we could have a *cava*: a cave where we could serve mezcal. Del Maguey threw the opening party for the event, an epic soiree. My dealer flew in three of the best bartenders from the US. There were two-hundred-fifty invites and two-hundred-fifty RSVPs. Security was tight to keep out crashers, but they were powerless to staunch the flow of hundreds of people jumping out of gondolas in the canal—men in formal tuxedos, women in backless dresses—to scale the fifteenth-century stone walls that barely contained the party. The energy and light and pheromones and music lifted me, I surfed the wave. A dead rockstar's widow was onstage, a rock goddess in her own right, red lipstick smeared as she crooned into the microphone. Italian fashion models mingled with art world giants, sophisticated collectors, and their beautiful young minions. Agnes B., the glamorous French fashion designer; James Turrell, one of my compadres in the Light and Space movement; and many old friends from the LA art scene were there—Peter Alexander, Billy Al Bengston, Laddie John Dill— sipping mezcal and letting the night take over. I took up residence behind the bar, pouring sips in clay copitas while Steve Olson, his associate Andy Seymour, and the lovely Misty Kalkofen, whose official title at Del Maguey is *madrina* (godmother) were shaking exquisite cocktails. Fellini's 8½ was projected onto the wall above us. After some time, I stepped out from behind the bar and pushed through the crowd, friends and strangers stopping me every few steps to press my hand or pull me in for a hug. One young man who stopped me I didn't recognize. Handsome and clean-cut, he was dressed in a tailored dark wool vest and smart black shirt. I'd never seen him before nor have I seen him since. As he shook my hand he leaned in to make himself heard over the raucousness of the party.

"I just want to say thank you," he said. "You changed my life." I never know what to say to this statement. I knew what he meant: that the mezcal, his introduction to it through Del Maguey and, by extension, me—that's what changed him. I hear it all the time. People I meet around the world confide in me how the mezcal transformed them. How it changed the way they drink, the way they live. The spirit can do that. Especially for those who have experienced where it comes from, the people who make it, and the role it has in Oaxacan culture. A sacred liquid. Drinking it connects you to a primordial force, the first deity.

It also connects you to the earth where it was made, the family who made it, the community they live in. How a spirit can transmit all that information is a mystery. But it can, I've witnessed it. People tell me they learned to take mezcal ceremonially, in gratitude. It's my greatest joy, to be able to share the spirit with people who appreciate the ritual of it. The young man at the party wanted to me to know he experienced mezcal as I do and was thankful for it. I smiled and answered him the only way I know how: "Cool, man."

THE COCKTAILS

There are two reasons I created Del Maguey: to preserve a piece of the culture in Oaxaca and to be able to share mezcal with my friends. Well, I have a lot more friends today than when I started. A good number of them I met through mezcal. Progressive chefs and bartenders have supported Del Maguey since the beginning. Back then, bartenders were clamoring for something new, a spirit that brought fresh and mind-blowing flavors. The first mezcal cocktails they made were simple. Mark Miller at the Coyote Cafe put a mezcal float on a margarita and called it The Smokin' Margarita. Jimmy Yeager, of Jimmy's in Aspen, made his own version and rechristened it Jimmy's Margarita. Using mezcal this way slowly introduced people to the spirit. It was a familiar way to present something utterly foreign. Jimmy, Mark, and my pal Steve Olson were the spirit's (and my) first champions in the US.

In the years that followed, Steve introduced me to some of the country's best bartenders, spirits writers, and aficionados. He seemed to know them all. In 2009, we brought sixteen of them down to Oaxaca so they could meet Del Maguey's producers and witness the culture firsthand. Each of them was given a bottle of Vida, which had not yet hit the market. They were given a task: take it home and experiment with it. It didn't take long for them to put mezcal cocktails on their menus. Others followed suit. Eventually, customers started demanding the spirit, and we soon found ourselves in the midst of a mezcal boom. In 2016, I was honored to receive the James Beard Award for Outstanding Wine, Beer, or Spirits Professional. (The Beards are the culinary world's Oscars.) I stood at the podium to accept my award and, instead of a rambling speech, simply rattled off the names of every single person I could think of to thank. The list of names—mezcal producers, basket weavers, copita makers, seed investors, dedicated bartenders, my family, my friends—went on for several minutes. I wanted them all to bask in the recognition with me.

Without the support of bartenders around the country and the world who were fond of our mezcal, Del Maguey would not be what it is today. Cocktails have become one of the gateways to mezcal, and they continue to push the spirit into exciting new spaces. This is just a sampling of some of the great creations by many of my favorite people.

MEZCAL COLLINS

BY RON COOPER

SERVES 1

Okay, this one's mine. I am not a bartender. In fact, besides mezcal, I don't really drink spirits. But I do enjoy fixing a cocktail for friends when they visit me at my home and studio in Taos. A finger-stirred mezcal Negroni usually does the trick. But a warm afternoon calls for a Mezcal Collins, herbaceous and refreshing.

2 ounces Del Maguey Santo Domingo Albarradas Single Village Mezcal

Soda water, to top

Pour the mezcal into a collins glass filled with ice and top with soda.

OAXACA OLD FASHIONED

BY PHIL WARD OF MAYAHUEL IN NEW YORK CITY, NEW YORK

SERVES 1

The Old Fashioned is probably the most riffed-on cocktail of all time. "A template" is what Phil calls it. He came up with the Oaxaca Old Fashioned one night during his tenure at the iconic New York bar Death & Co, probably when some customer asked him to make something up on the spot. "It's not brain science," he says. "It's just a reposado tequila Old Fashioned, but with half an ounce of mezcal added to it. It's one of those things that outperformed the simplicity of the ingredients."

Mezcal pretty much took over Phil's life when he opened Mayahuel, the game-changing agave spirits bar in New York. He'd intended it to be a tequila bar. But every time he came up with a new tequila cocktail, he kept thinking how much better it would be with just a little mezcal in it. When he finally came to Oaxaca with me, he says, "It was pretty much game-over. That was my big epiphany moment. I was with Ron, Misty [Kalkofen], and Steve [Olson] and I remember thinking, *This is the purest spirit I've ever tasted.* I realized then what the difference was between mezcal and every other spirit out there. The people who make it, they've been making this stuff longer than they can remember. And they've been making this mezcal as delicious as possible, because they intended to drink every bit of it themselves with their family and friends."

1½ ounces reposado tequila

½ ounce Del Maguey Chichicapa Single Village Mezcal

1 teaspoon agave nectar

1 dash Angostura bitters

1 wide swath of orange peel, for garnish

Combine all the ingredients, except the garnish, in a mixing glass filled with ice and stir until well chilled. Strain into a rocks glass over one large ice cube. In one hand, hold a lighted match over the drink and, in the other hand, hold the orange peel, with the orange side facing the flame about an inch away. Carefully and quickly squeeze the orange peel until its oils spark, then drop the peel into the cocktail.

CIGAR BOX

BY JUSTIN LAVENUE OF THE ROOSEVELT ROOM IN AUSTIN, TEXAS
SERVES 1

Texas is an old-fashioned drinking state, as in an Old Fashioned drinking state. Justin's variation on that classic cocktail plays up the smoky notes in the mezcal with a smoked tea syrup and tobacco essence. It's the top-selling drink at The Roosevelt Room and has acquired something of a cult following around Austin. Using vanilla bean, cocoa nibs, and coffee beans, Justin came up with a clever and elegant tincture that evokes the essence of cigar.

2 ounces Del Maguey Vida Single Village Mezcal

¼ ounce Lapsang Souchong syrup (recipe below)

3 dashes Scrappy's Lavender Bitters

3 dashes homemade tobacco essence (recipe below)

1 cinnamon stick, for garnish

Combine all the ingredients, except the garnish, in an old-fashioned glass with one large ice cube and stir until well chilled. Burn one end of the cinnamon stick until it starts to smoke and place it next to (but not inside!) the drink on a glass ashtray to serve.

LAPSANG SOUCHONG SYRUP

Steep 1 cup of loose lapsang souchong tea in 4 cups of simmering water for 10 minutes, stirring intermittently. Strain off the tea using a fine strainer. Measure the volume of the liquid, then add an equal volume of sugar (1:1 ratio). Stir well to dissolve all the sugar, then bottle. Keep refrigerated between uses for up to two weeks.

TOBACCO ESSENCE

Combine one bottle of El Dorado 5 Year Rum, ¾ cup black tea leaves, ⅛ cup (2 tablespoons) black tea leaves scorched with a culinary torch, ¼ cup cocoa nibs, ¼ cup ground coffee beans, ¼ cup crushed hazelnuts, 1 ounce (by weight) Demerara sugar, 1 ounce Plantation O.F.T.D. Rum, 1 tablespoon vanilla extract, and 1 tablespoon quassia bark chips and stir well until sugar is dissolved and other ingredients are incorporated. Macerate for 24 hours, shaking vigorously every 8 hours. Strain through a coffee filter to remove all solids and bottle. Store indefinitely.

LA VIDA BUENA

BY STEVE OLSON, GLOBAL MEZCAL ADVOCATE

SERVES 1

Steve Olson and I have always loved mezcal Negronis. Our friend and the amazing bartender Jacques Bezuidenhout made the first one with Tobala. Steve and his team at aka wine geek, the consulting firm he ran for twenty-five years, took it upon themselves to make a true mezcal Negroni. It took a lot of recipe testing, but they finally nailed down this two-one-one formula that switched out Campari for its softer, sweeter cousin Aperol. They called it La Vida Buena: The Good Life. Because that's how you feel when you're drinking it—that life is good.

For Del Maguey's twentieth anniversary, La Vida Buena was served not only at the party in Oaxaca but also at bars around the world—132 bars in seventeen nations, to be precise. After that, the drink became something of a phenomenon. It was posted all over social media. At one point, Steve said he knew of at least thirty bars around the world that had it on the menu.

Steve and I still love to drink mezcal Negronis together. I can't count the number of Vida Buenas that have kicked off amazing nights, unforgettable meals, conversations that last all night. I'm honored that he helped me introduce mezcal to the world's bartenders.

1½ ounces Del Maguey Vida Single Village Mezcal

¾ ounce Carpano Antica

¾ ounce Aperol

3 dashes Regan's Orange Bitters

1 wide swath of orange peel, for garnish

Combine all the ingredients, except the garnish, in a mixing glass filled with ice and stir until well chilled. Strain into a rocks glass over one large ice cube. Garnish with the orange peel.

THE BRAVE

BY BOBBY HEUGEL OF ANVIL BAR & REFUGE IN HOUSTON, TEXAS
SERVES 1

I met Bobby Heugel a decade ago when I walked into the bar he was tending at the time. I looked him right in the eyes, without saying hello, and told him, "You need to try this," as I swung a bottle of Chichicapa before him like a pendulum on a grandfather clock.

I had two bottles of mezcal with me that day: Chichicapa and Tobala. I remember watching Bobby as he tasted the Chichicapa. "It shattered everything I thought I knew about agave spirits," he says. And of the Tobala, "The finish lasted forever, to the point where I was dumbfounded that a spirit could be so bold, yet so nuanced. I had never tasted anything like that in my life. In short, Ron made tequila somewhat boring for me in less than ten minutes and sparked a curiosity in me for what else I misunderstood about Mexico." Over the next few years, Bobby drank every mezcal he could get his hands on and started traveling to Mexico regularly—more than fifty times since our first meeting. Today, he owns a *mezcalería* in Houston, as well as several other bars stocked to the brim with great mezcals.

"I developed this cocktail because it reflects how I like to drink my mezcal—undiluted," he says of The Brave, which should be served at room temperature, without ice.

1¼ ounces Del Maguey Chichicapa Single Village Mezcal

¾ ounce blanco tequila (preferably from the Highlands)

½ ounce Averna Amaro

¼ ounce Grand Marnier

3 mists Angostura bitters

1 wide swath of orange peel, for garnish

In a wineglass, combine all the ingredients, except the bitters and orange peel, without ice and swirl gently. Mist three small bursts of bitters onto the surface of the cocktail and along the inner sides of the glass. In one hand, hold a lighted match over the drink and, in the other hand, the orange peel, with the orange side facing the flame about an inch away. Carefully and quickly squeeze the orange peel until its oils spark, then drop the peel into the cocktail.

SINGLE VILLAGE FIX

BY THAD VOGLER OF BAR AGRICOLE AND TROU NORMAND
IN SAN FRANCISCO, CALIFORNIA
SERVES 1

This cocktail was created by Thad Vogler, who was something of a mentor in the San Francisco bar scene. The guys who worked with him referred to it as the "Double Village Fix" because the drink was so damn good that whenever somebody ordered one, they'd automatically make two just so they could split the other one. The rare and wonderful thing about this cocktail is that it allows the mezcal to shine. Using a different mezcal completely changes the flavor of the drink, so I highly encourage experimentation. It's delicious with Minero or San Luis del Río, and out of this world with our Espadin Especial. The drink works as a showcase for the mezcal and a valuable tool to show just how unique each expression is.

1½ ounces Del Maguey Chichicapa Single Village Mezcal

1 ounce Small Hand Foods Pineapple Gum Syrup

¾ ounce freshly squeezed lime juice

Combine all the ingredients in a cocktail shaker filled with ice and shake until well chilled. Strain into a chilled coupe and serve with no garnish.

MAXIMILIAN AFFAIR

BY MISTY KALKOFEN, MADRINA FOR DEL MAGUEY
SERVES 1

When Misty Kalkofen was studying theology at Harvard Divinity School, she worked as a bartender—a job she loved. At the end of her program, she had a choice: pursue a PhD or keep bartending. Much to the chagrin of her parents, she decided to keep working behind the bar. I met her the night she created this drink, which was also the first time she ever tasted mezcal. That night, I told her about the spirit's ritual use in Oaxaca.

"It was like my two worlds coming together," Misty likes to say. Less than a year later, we were in Oaxaca together. In Santa Catarina Minas, I told Don Lencho that Misty had studied religion. The old man said, "She must bless the roast then." Together, Misty and Don Lencho climbed the mound of maguey and stuck a wooden cross in it. Misty said, "Right after, I boarded a van headed for the airport and cried my eyes out. I feel fortunate—not a lot of people can look back on a single moment and say, 'That's when my life changed.'" As soon as Del Maguey could afford it, we hired Misty to be our East Coast *juez*. (Other companies use the title "brand ambassador," but I like juez, referring to the ceremonial role of pouring mezcal for others.) After a few years, she graduated to madrina, or godmother, a title she chose for herself.

"Working for Del Maguey is a dream come true," Misty says, to my delight. "The term *Guelaguetza* (as in, the annual festival) refers to a complementary exchange. What we have with our palenqueros is a reciprocal relationship. They offer us the chance to learn about their culture and provide us with this amazing product, which, in turn, gives them opportunities to improve the lives of their families and villages. I feel whole and happy when I'm in Oaxaca."

1 ounce Del Maguey Chichicapa Single Village Mezcal

1 ounce St-Germain elderflower liqueur

½ ounce Punt e Mes

½ ounce freshly squeezed lemon juice

1 wide swath of lemon peel, for garnish

Combine all the ingredients, except the garnish, in a cocktail shaker filled with ice. Shake vigorously until well chilled, then let the shaker rest until condensation forms on the outside. Strain into an old-fashioned glass over one large ice cube. Garnish with the lemon peel.

PONCHE DE MEZCAL PARA EL AÑO NUEVO

BY STEVE OLSON, GLOBAL MEZCAL ADVOCATE
SERVES 8

The Oaxacan Dream was one of the first-ever mezcal cocktails. Steve Olson created it with Leo DeGroff and Andy Seymour, his compadres at aka wine geek. It was so simple, yet so beautiful—mezcal, pineapple juice, cranberry, lime, and agave nectar, but the juice was freshly pressed and the drink came with a grilled pineapple garnish. We loved the drink, but after a few years, it began to feel pretty basic compared to the amazing cocktails bartenders around the country were coming up with. So, Steve did what any rational bartender would do: He turned it into a punch. The Ponche de Mezcal para el Año Nuevo (Mezcal Punch for the New Year) was first served at my art opening at Franklin Parrasch Gallery in New York. Forget the bad white wine they usually serve at these events. We had this beautiful punch and everyone there—bartenders who came and art-world people alike—loved it.

OLEO-SACCHARUM

8 lemons

4 pink grapefruit

2 cups Demerara sugar

PUNCH

1 bottle (25 ounces) Del Maguey Vida Single Village Mezcal

6 ounces Dos Maderas PX 5+5 Rum

10 ounces Dry Sack Medium Sherry

10 ounces hibiscus tea

12 ounces freshly squeezed lemon juice

16 ounces freshly squeezed pink grapefruit juice

16 ounces fresh pineapple juice

10 ounces fresh unsweetened pomegranate juice

12 dashes Angostura bitters

Whole nutmeg, for garnish

16 ounces cava, to top

1 grapefruit, sliced, for garnish

To make the oleo-saccharum, peel the lemons and grapefruit, working in a circular pattern around the fruit to make long, twisting peels. Reserve the fruit for the punch. Combine the peels with the Demerara sugar at the bottom of a punch bowl and muddle the peels into the sugar. Cover the bowl with plastic wrap and leave overnight.

The next day, stir the mixture, which should be a paste of sugar and peels. Squeeze the juice from the reserved lemons and grapefruit into the oleo-saccharum and stir to create the base for the punch.

To make the punch, add the mezcal, rum, sherry, hibiscus tea, and lemon, grapefruit, pineapple, and pomegranate juices and stir. Add the bitters and grate fresh nutmeg over the punch bowl. Add an ice block or several large ice cubes and garnish with slices of grapefruit. Ladle into small punch cups (teacups are perfect) over one or two ice cubes, top with cava, and grate more nutmeg over the top of each cup.

NAKED AND FAMOUS

BY JOAQUÍN SIMÓ OF POURING RIBBONS IN NEW YORK CITY, NEW YORK

SERVES 1

Joaquín Simó came up with this drink when he worked at the seminal cocktail bar Death & Co. He'd been introduced to mezcal through his colleague Phil Ward, who had just created the Oaxaca Old Fashioned (page 206).

"I tasted it and was just floored," Joaquín recalls of Phil's drink. "I had no idea you could get flavors like that. Three expressions of agave in the glass . . . it was one of the best things I'd ever put in my mouth. There was very little mezcal being brought in at the time. A lot of it still came in bottles with the *gusano* or worm (really, moth larva) at the bottom. But there was Del Maguey."

He started playing around with it and came up with Naked and Famous, which he describes as "the bastard love child of a classic Last Word and a Paper Plane (by Sam Ross of the New York cocktail den Attaboy), conceived in the mountains of Oaxaca." He says that using a big, funky mezcal like Chichicapa was key to stand up to two complex liqueurs. The four ingredients, in equal parts, create a harmony.

¾ ounce Del Maguey Chichicapa Single Village Mezcal

¾ ounce Yellow Chartreuse Liqueur

¾ ounce Aperol

¾ ounce freshly squeezed lime juice

Combine all the ingredients in a cocktail shaker filled with ice and shake until well chilled. Strain into a chilled coupe and serve with no garnish.

MEZCAL MULE

BY JIM MEEHAN OF PDT IN NEW YORK CITY, NEW YORK

SERVES 1

Jim Meehan originally developed this recipe for another brand, Sombra Mezcal, which was started by a sommelier named Richard Betts. Before launching his company, Betts came to me for advice about how to enter the business and work with palenqueros. I helped set him up with the necessary contacts he needed in Oaxaca and even introduced him to Paciano Cruz Nolasco and his son, Marcos, from San Luis del Río. Betts asked for my okay to source his mezcal from them. Sombra eventually switched palenques, but Jim always preferred this drink with the mezcal from San Luis. So, when we started producing Vida there, the Mezcal Mule became a Vida cocktail. It goes to show that each mezcal is unique. You can't necessarily use them interchangeably. The Mezcal Mule is designed to hit every note—sweet, tart, floral, hot, smoky. It best achieves this with the floral, fruity, and spiced Vida Single Village Mezcal.

3 cucumber slices (plus 1 for garnish)

½ ounce agave nectar

1½ ounces Del Maguey Vida Single Village Mezcal

1 ounce ginger beer

¾ ounce freshly squeezed lime juice

¾ ounce passion fruit puree, preferably Boiron brand

1 piece candied ginger, for garnish

1 pinch ground chile, for garnish

Muddle the 3 cucumber slices and agave nectar in a cocktail shaker, and then add all the remaining ingredients, except the garnishes. Shake with ice, then fine-strain into a chilled rocks glass over ice. Garnish with a piece of candied ginger and a slice of cucumber on a toothpick and a pinch of ground chile.

LA OTRA PALABRA

BY ERIC ALPERIN OF THE VARNISH, BAR CLACSON, AND THE SLIPPER CLUTCH
IN LOS ANGELES, CALIFORNA, AND HALF STEP IN AUSTIN, TEXAS

SERVES 1

Eric Alperin came up with this variation on the Last Word, a classic cocktail, after traveling to Oaxaca and getting his first bottle of Vida. One day during the trip, we were sitting in the bodega together after a long day riding around in the van visiting palenques and tasting mezcal. We were sitting on crates of bottles, watching the bottling line, shooting the shit. Eric turned to me and said, "Wow, man. It's so simple." And I knew: he got it. "Yeah!" I replied. "And it *works*, man!"

Eric and I are simpatico. We both started as artists. Eric was an actor, and he studied theater. We run our projects in similar ways; it's important for him that each member of his staff feels a sense of ownership of the bar. "Ron is a Yoda" Eric likes to say. "It helps that he kinda looks like a Zapotec, too." I like that. Eric and I, we understand each other.

2 ounces Del Maguey Vida Single Village Mezcal

¼ ounce Luxardo Maraschino Liqueur

¼ ounce Yellow Chartreuse Liqueur

1 ounce freshly squeezed lime juice

1 generous bar spoon agave nectar

Combine all the ingredients in a cocktail shaker and add ice last. Shake until well chilled. Strain into a rocks glass over a large rock (or, in bar parlance, a BFIC: big fucking ice cube) and serve with no garnish.

LA ESMERALDA

BY RYAN MAYBEE OF MANIFESTO IN KANSAS CITY, MISSOURI
SERVES 1

Ryan Maybee is a partner in a company called J. Rieger & Company, a Kansas City brand that was around back in the 1800s but died with Prohibition; it was recently resurrected. One of their products is a coffee amaro. It marries beautifully with Vida. He named the cocktail for La Esmeralda, a region in Oaxaca known for producing great coffee beans.

When he opened his bar, Manifesto, in 2009, Ryan wanted to serve Del Maguey. Sadly, it wasn't yet available in Missouri. He took it upon himself to bring it in, and when he finally succeeded, we ended up having the local launch party at his bar. Since then, Ryan says, mezcal has become something of a bartender's secret handshake in Kansas City. It's getting to be popular with consumers, too. But you still run into people all the time who have never heard of mezcal. Ryan loves to be the one to introduce it to them.

1 ounce Del Maguey Vida Single Village Mezcal

1 ounce J. Rieger & Company Caffè Amaro

½ ounce Cocchi Vermouth di Torino

¼ ounce Ancho Reyes Chili Liqueur

4 drops Bittermens Xocolatl Mole Bitters

1 wide swath of orange peel, for garnish

Combine all the ingredients, except the garnish, in a mixing glass filled with ice and stir until well chilled. Strain into a rocks glass over one large ice cube. Garnish with the orange peel.

QUICKSAND

BY RYAN FITZGERALD OF ABV AND OVER PROOF IN SAN FRANCISCO, CALIFORNIA

SERVES 1

Ryan Fitzgerald, who worked for Del Maguey as our West Coast juez, had this idea that mezcal would work well in a Scotch cocktail. Mezcal can be smoky, like certain Scotches, so he thought, *Let's swap the Scotch out for mezcal and see what happens.* He decided to try it with a Scotch cocktail he's never really liked. "The Blood and Sand is a drink that's never made sense to me," he explains. "None of the recipes I've seen really work. But I like the idea behind it. So, I started tinkering. The funny thing was that I already had the name. Quicksand was so perfect that I *had* to get the drink to work. It was in production for a long time. We finally tweaked it just right and it's been on the menu at ABV ever since."

Before getting into mezcal, Ryan was a tequila aficionado. He'd been to a number of distilleries, but nothing prepared him for his first trip to Oaxaca. "To see these tiny palenques making the most amazing spirit in the middle of nowhere, to eat amazing mole in these humble altar rooms, the whole experience changed my life," he says. "When I got home, I just couldn't stop talking about it. Here I was, having grown up in Southern California, I was fluent in Spanish, I went surfing in Mexico all the time. But I didn't realize how much Mexican culture had been speaking to me my whole life until I found mezcal—or, as Ron would put it, until mezcal found me."

1½ ounces Del Maguey Vida Single Village Mezcal

¾ ounce Pierre Ferrand Dry Curaçao

¾ ounce Maurin Quina

4 dashes orange bitters

1 wide swath of orange peel, for garnish

Combine all the ingredients, except the garnish, in a mixing glass filled with ice and stir. Strain into a chilled cocktail glass. Garnish with the orange peel.

DUSTY ROADS

BY ERIK LORINCZ OF THE SAVOY IN LONDON, ENGLAND

SERVES 1

For this cocktail, Erik Lorincz explains, he wanted to capture the dreamy pleasure of day-time drinking. There was a good deal of that activity on the trip he took to Oaxaca with me and Steve Olson several years ago. He named the drink for the treasured moments we spent driving from village to village, talking about everything under the sun. Dusty Roads is floral, refreshing, and a little lighter in alcohol than many mezcal cocktails are.

Erik describes his experiences with mezcal beautifully: "Mezcal is a spirit that got me right away, the first time I tasted it. I'd tried the kind with the worm in it, both in London and Slovakia, where I'm from. I don't count those times. My true mezcal moment was at a mezcalería in Mexico City. I took my first sip and instantly loved it. No other spirit ever got me on the first sip. I thought, *This is the real nectar of gods.* I felt privileged to taste something so rare, so complex. It's so rustic, yet so well made. No electric tools, everything by hand. When I was in Oaxaca, I met Faustino in Chichicapa. When I shook his hand, I felt his palm and asked if I could take a closer look. It was covered in scars, so rough. He must have thought it strange of me to ask, but he let me take a picture of it. It was the hand of a true artisan."

1 ounce Cocchi Americano Rosa

¾ ounce Del Maguey Tobala

3 dashes Peychaud's Bitters

¼ ounce lemon verbena cordial (recipe below)

Roasted chapulines (grasshoppers), for garnish

Combine all the ingredients, except the garnish, in a mixing glass filled with ice and stir. Strain into a rocks glass over ice and garnish with roasted chapulines.

LEMON VERBENA CORDIAL

Chop lemon verbena leaves and gently muddle them in a bowl. Combine 1 part of the muddled leaves with 2 parts sugar and 2 parts water in a saucepan over medium-high heat and stir until the sugar is dissolved. Stir in the lemon verbena leaves and remove from the heat. Let the mixture steep and cool for half an hour, then bottle, strain, and refrigerate for up to 1 week.

ANDRÉS Y COOPER

BY MIGUEL LANCHA OF JOSÉ ANDRÉS'S THINKFOODGROUP IN WASHINGTON, DC
SERVES 1

The idea for this cocktail was born of an assignment from José Andrés. He wanted his staff to create a drink to pair with a tapa made with jamón Ibérico. They ended up combining the drink and the tapa in one: the tapa became the garnish, a slice of jamón Ibérico and a black Kalamata olive macerated in herbs. Of course, there's also Ibérico in the liquid because it's made with Del Maguey Ibérico. It's not a mezcal that often gets used in cocktails.

The drink was named "Andrés y Cooper" as a tribute to the friendship José and I formed. The mezcal represents me and the sherry represents him. While writing this book, I learned that the ever-innovative team at ThinkFoodGroup is experimenting again with Del Maguey Ibérico, aging the mezcal in a goat leather bag, a traditional Spanish wineskin called a *botarrón*. I can only fathom what the result will be, but I'm sure José and Miguel, the group's official "cocktail innovator," will use it to make something fantastic.

¾ ounce Del Maguey Ibérico

¾ ounce Yzaguirre 1884 Sweet Vermouth

¾ ounce Hidalgo Napoleón Amontillado Sherry

½ ounce Cynar

1 pinch kosher salt

1 wide swath of orange peel

1 Kalamata olive

1 thin slice jamón Ibérico

Combine the mezcal, vermouth, sherry, Cynar, and salt in a mixing glass with ice and stir until well chilled. Strain into a double old-fashioned glass over one large ice cube. For the garnish, hold the orange peel aloft and express the oil by gently squeezing it, then rub the peel around the rim of the glass and discard. Spear the olive and jamón with a cocktail pick, place it on the rim, and serve.

GALLO DE ORO

BY SEBASTIEN GANS OF CANDELARIA IN PARIS, FRANCE
SERVES 1

The first mezcal that Carina Soto Velasquez, co-owner of the game-changing cocktail bar Candelaria in Paris, tasted was Del Maguey Chichicapa from a plastic water bottle. I was in Paris for FIAC (Foire International d'Art Contemporain)—not for mezcal, but for art—and a mutual distributor friend introduced us. Carina was instantly fascinated with mezcal. When American friends would visit her, she would always ask that they bring her Del Maguey.

Before Candelaria, there were not many places serving mezcal in Paris. Today, the spirit's popularity has grown. But there is still a lot of room for discovery. "For the French, it helps to communicate mezcal's relationship to wine," Carina says. "We explain to customers about the different regions, the different varieties. When you start talking about it this way, people get curious and are able to better understand the spirit. The concept of terroir is already a part of the culture here."

1 ounce coffee-infused Vida (recipe below)

1 ounce Vermouth Del Professore Bianco

1 teaspoon Pierre Ferrand Dry Curaçao

½ teaspoon Peter Heering Cherry Liqueur

1 spritz oloroso sherry, for aromatics

1 Amarena cherry, for garnish

Combine the coffee-infused vida, vermouth, curaçao, and cherry liqueur in a mixing glass filled with ice and stir until well chilled. Strain into a small coupe. Spritz with sherry and garnish with the cherry.

COFFEE-INFUSED VIDA

Combine 1 tablespoon ground coffee (a robust dark roast from Kenya, Uganda, or Rwanda) with 1 bottle of Del Maguey Vida Single Village Mezcal and let steep for no more than 5 minutes. Filter through a Superbag or other ultrafine strainer. Store indefinitely.

MEZCALERO

BY JOHN LERMAYER OF SWEET LIBERTY IN MIAMI BEACH, FLORIDA
SERVES 1

John's trip to Oaxaca is what inspired the Mezcalero. He first started thinking up the recipe while he was there, seeing the place where Del Maguey is made. He wanted to make something beautiful, and I believe he succeeded. He's a beautiful guy, the way he puts things—like when he talks about his first experience with mezcal: "My introduction to mezcal was through Ron, although neither of us knew it at the time. When I discovered mezcal, it was his mezcal. But I wouldn't meet him until some years later. Knowing Ron has changed a lot of us in this business. The success he's achieved was never supposed to happen to him. It wasn't the goal when he embarked on his journey. Mezcal is something that found him. For many of us, it validates this idea of following your heart. I believe the world is a better place knowing that Ron Cooper has lived in it. I feel lucky to be his friend."

Like I said, a beautiful guy.

1 ounce Del Maguey Vida Single Village Mezcal

1 ounce Aperol

1 ounce blanc vermouth

1 wide swath of grapefruit peel, for garnish

Combine all the ingredients, except the garnish, in a cocktail shaker filled with ice and shake until chilled. Strain into an old-fashioned glass over one large ice cube. Garnish with the grapefruit peel.

BONFIRE OF THE VANITIES

BY ERYN REECE OF THE WOOLY PUBLIC IN NEW YORK CITY, NEW YORK
SERVES 1

Eryn was with me in Oaxaca for one of those mezcal-finds-you moments. I took a bunch of friends down for Faustino's son, Maximino's, wedding in Chichicapa. Afterward, the group parted ways. I took those who stayed on to visit a couple of new producers I was hoping to add. Eryn wasn't prepared for the kind of adventuring we did in Oaxaca, especially all the driving—always on roads that are barely roads, way up in the mountains. She's afraid of heights. And I'd just quit smoking, so I wasn't as laid-back as usual. At one point, in the driver's seat, feeling a craving for a cigarette come on, I yelled, "I need mezcal!" Someone poured me a little, and there I was, driving with one hand holding the copita and the other barely steering the wheel. I glanced over at Eryn and saw that she was terrified. I told her, "When we get there and it's stunning and you get to sip straight-off-the-still mezcal at the source, you'll see. It's worth it."

Eryn uses two of her favorite ingredients in this drink: mezcal and sherry. They're a natural pairing. The cocktail plays up the nuttiness of the sherry and the smokiness of mezcal. The coffee liqueur and mole bitters are a nod to Oaxacan culture.

1½ ounces Del Maguey Vida Single Village Mezcal

¾ ounce Lustau Amontillado Sherry

½ ounce Carpano Antica

½ ounce Caffé Lolita Coffee Liqueur

½ ounce Ancho Reyes Chili Liqueur

1 dash Bittermens Xocolatl Mole Bitters

Combine all the ingredients in a mixing glass filled with ice and stir until well chilled. Strain into a chilled Nick & Nora glass and serve with no garnish.

ESPERANTO

BY JACKSON CANNON OF THE HAWTHORNE IN BOSTON, MASSACHUSETTS
SERVES 1

Jackson has always been fascinated by Esperanto, this language created from several others to unite the people of the world. It fits here because a couple of different languages are being spoken in this cocktail. Jackson created it one night at The Hawthorne for a party that kept requesting mezcal drinks. He remembers looking up at the green wall of bottles and trying to come up with something new. Almost by accident, he grabbed Del Maguey Crema, a mezcal with agave nectar built right into it. When it first came out, bartenders weren't using Crema as a cocktail base. It was more of a training-wheels sipper. In this drink, Crema gets top billing. Jackson wasn't sure how the drink would turn out, but when he tasted it, he couldn't get over the body. It was just so fat!

Jackson came down to Oaxaca, and the experience, he said, was life-changing. He sat on the floor, drinking straight from the still in Minas with a couple of other guys, just weeping. It was too beautiful, he said. Steve Olson was there, and seeing these guys in a weird emotional place, he asked if they were okay. All Jackson could manage as a response was, "Can we pay more for this? We want to pay more." In that moment, they were struck by how precious the spirit was, how much it needed to be cherished. He described it as a spiritual experience and saw how the Oaxaqueños were my people—like when I was telling him, "Back when your motherfucking *ancestors* were moving *stones* from one pile to another to fucking *count*, man, *my* people (as in, the Mayas) were inventing *zero*!" He laughed. He totally got it.

2 ounces Del Maguey Crema de Mezcal

¾ ounce La Cigarrera Manzanilla Sherry

½ ounce Carpano Antica

1 dash Regan's Orange Bitters

1 wide swath of lemon peel, for garnish

Combine all the ingredients, except the garnish, in a mixing glass filled with ice and stir until well chilled. Strain into a double old-fashioned glass over one large ice cube. Garnish with lemon oil by rubbing the peel over the rim of the glass inside, then discard it.

FADE TO BLACK

BY JEREMY OERTEL OF DEATH & CO IN NEW YORK, NEW YORK
SERVES 1

In the summer of 2017, I made a last-minute trip to New York for a party. It was for Mayahuel's last night. It's been said before: this bar was a game changer. It helped shape the way people see agave spirits and, particularly, mezcal. Owner Phil Ward had intended to open a tequila bar. But he never felt the need to stock every tequila out there. And the more mezcal he tasted, the more space it occupied on the shelves.

Like me, Jeremy was a fan of Mayahuel—long before he ever worked there. After Phil invited him to get behind the bar, he promptly fell in love with mezcal. "Back then, everybody was so curious about it," he says. "I loved sharing it with people. And I loved being a part of the place that started it all for a lot of people."

1 ounce Del Maguey Vida Single Village Mezcal

1 ounce Ramazzotti Amaro

¼ ounce Smith & Cross Jamaican Rum

2 dashes of Bittermens Xocolatl Mole Bitters

Pinch of salt

1 whole egg

Negra Modelo, to top

Combine all the ingredients, except the Modelo Negra, in a cocktail shaker without ice and dry shake (without ice). Add ice and shake until well chilled. Strain into a collins glass and top with Negra Modelo.

CALL RON COOPER

BY ALEX KRATENA AND SIMONE CAPORALE OF P(OUR) IN LONDON, ENGLAND
SERVES 1

One night at Artesian, the hotel bar at The Langham Hotel, a bunch of American bartenders burst through the front door. They were in town for World Class, the international bartending competition. Charles Joly, of the Aviary in Chicago, had won. Alex suddenly found himself hosting an after-party. As the story goes, Charles asked for a refreshing drink made with tequila or mezcal, so Simone and Alex made him a huge swizzle with an over-the-top garnish that included a naked Barbie doll and vintage-looking phone earpiece. The final touch was a copita of Tobala (courtesy of Steve Olson, who was in the house that night). Just as Alex was serving Charles the drink, Steve's phone rang. It was me calling! They quickly plugged the earpiece into a phone and passed it to Charles, so I could congratulate him on the win. And that's how the drink got its name.

1¾ ounces blanco tequila

1 ounce Del Maguey San Luis del Río Single Village Mezcal

1 ounce Velvet Falernum Liqueur

½ ounce freshly squeezed lime juice

3 dashes Peychaud's Bitters

1 tablespoon agave nectar

Combine all the ingredients in a highball glass, and then fill it nearly halfway with crushed ice. Using a swizzle stick, swizzle the drink to chill. Top off with more crushed ice and garnish absurdly.

DONAJI

BY JULIAN COX OF THREE DOTS AND A DASH IN CHICAGO, ILLINOIS
SERVES 1

The legend of Donaji is Mexico's very own Romeo and Juliet story about a Zapotec princess who falls in love with a prince from a rival Mixtec clan. She ends up offering herself up as a hostage to the Mixtecs, but later, when the Zapotecs try to save her, she's decapitated. Julian loves this story and wanted the cocktail to be as pretty and exotic as Princess Donaji herself. He had the idea of dropping pomegranate pearls in the drink, red dots of color. It's garnished with lemon leaves and a salt made with *chapulines*—grasshoppers.

What makes the drink special is that you can substitute another mezcal for the Chichicapa, which changes the flavor profile. It was originally made with Santo Domingo Albarradas—its tropical fruit flavors complemented the exotic flavors in the drink. One day, Julian made one for me. I never tell these guys how to do their job, but this time I had an idea: "Man, try it with Pechuga." We danced around the restaurant after we tried it.

Chapulín salt (recipe below), for rimming the glass

2 ounces Del Maguey Chichicapa Single Village Mezcal

⅜ ounce freshly squeezed lime juice (equal to 2¼ teaspoons)

⅜ ounce freshly squeezed lemon juice

1 ounce freshly squeezed orange juice

¾ ounce agave nectar

Pomegranate seeds, for garnish

2 lime wheels, for garnish

1 lemon leaf, for garnish

Rim a double rocks glass with chapulín salt. Combine all the ingredients, except the garnishes, in a cocktail shaker filled with ice and shake until well chilled. Strain into the prepared rocks glass over ice. Garnish with the pomegranate seeds, lime wheels, and lemon leaf.

CHAPULÍN SALT

Finely chop dried chapulines (grasshoppers). Mix with an equal quantity of rock salt.

CATRINA

BY MARC ALVAREZ SAFONT OF NIÑO VIEJO AND THE ELBARRI GROUP
IN BARCELONA, SPAIN
SERVES 1

For the longest time, they could not get mezcal in Spain. There weren't many importers bringing in Mexican products, aside from the gusano stuff with the so-called "worm" at the bottom of the bottle. When Del Maguey became available, bartenders went crazy for it. But they had to come up with ways to make it approachable for the average customer who had never tasted it before. Marc's idea was a variation on sangrita, the nonalcoholic beverage traditionally served with tequila. He did it as a long drink, served over crushed ice, that uses chamoy, a Mexican condiment made from fermented fruits that you can find in any Mexican food shop. In this drink, the chamoy is used in a syrup, like grenadine. The drink comes with a little clay copita of mezcal as a garnish. But really, the mezcal is more than a garnish. The sangrita is served with the mezcal—not quite as a chaser, more as a pairing—both to refresh the palate and to harmonize with the spirit. Should you decide to pour the mezcal into the sangrita, that works as well. The result is a refreshing cocktail. It's really up to the imbiber to decide.

4 ounces apricot juice

½ ounce freshly squeezed lime juice

1 ounce freshly squeezed orange juice

1¼ ounces chamoy syrup (recipe below)

1½ ounces Del Maguey Chichicapa Single Village Mezcal

Combine all the fruit juices in a highball glass filled with crushed ice and swizzle. Top up with more ice and drizzle the chamoy syrup over top. Pour the mezcal into a copita and place it on the edge of the glass to serve.

CHAMOY SYRUP

Heat water in the bottom of a double boiler. When it reaches the boiling point, pour 2 ounces chamoy and 3 cups simple syrup into the top part of the double boiler, and mix well until the chamoy is completely dissolved. Store in the refrigerator for up to 2 days.

MEZCAL CIDER RICKEY

BY CHRIS BOSTICK OF HALF STEP IN AUSTIN, TEXAS
SERVES 1

Growing up in Texas with its huge Mexican population, Chris had tried mezcal. But it was the adulterated stuff with the gusano. When he tasted it, he thought, *Holy shit. That's strong.* He pretty much swore off it and just stuck to tequila until he was introduced to Del Maguey.

"That first taste of Chichicapa changed everything," he says. "I got behind it right away."

When he came to Oaxaca with me, I asked him, "Man, have you ever seen a tobalá?" He and the other guys on the trip were sitting on the bus, passing around bottles. I was up front by myself, all quiet. Then, all of a sudden, I started pointing out the plants as we passed them. *TOH-ba-LAH. TOH-ba-LAH. TOH-ba-LAH.* Like a chant. Chris and the others started whipping their heads around, looking out the window, trying to get a glimpse. When they saw the maguey in the wild like that and started to be able to tell one variety from another, that's when it started to become, like, *Ah. Now I get it.*

2 ounces Del Maguey Vida Single Village Mezcal

¾ ounce honey syrup (page 242)

¾ ounce freshly squeezed lime juice

2½ to 3 ounces apple cider, to top

1 lime wheel, to garnish

Combine the mezcal, honey syrup, and lime juice in a cocktail shaker filled with crushed ice and give it a "whip and dump," which is like a half shake. (Because you're topping with cider, you don't want to shake too vigorously and dilute the drink.) Strain into a collins glass over ice and top with cider. Give it a nice stir and garnish with the lime wheel.

TIA MIA

BY IVY MIX OF LEYENDA IN BROOKLYN, NEW YORK
SERVES 1

Ivy wouldn't be in the cocktail world were it not for mezcal. She was an art student when she moved to Guatemala at nineteen and started hanging out at a mezcal bar in Antigua. This was before Facebook and smartphones. If you wanted to meet people, you went to the bar. This particular bar let her run up a sizable tab, and then let her bartend there to work it off. Ivy's love of mezcal is second only to her wanderlust. While working in a mezcal bar, she started traveling to Mexico and learning more about the spirit. She would smuggle bottles back to Guatemala for her boss.

As a younger bartender, Ivy put mezcal in everything. With the Tia Mia, she thought, *Oh, a mai tai is delicious. It will be even more delicious with mezcal.* And it was.

"I do miss the art world, though," she says. "Being with Ron makes me miss it more. We talk about our favorite artists. Half the people I studied in school he knows personally. When we're together now, we don't even talk about mezcal. We drink it, but what we're talking about is art, life, everything."

1 ounce Del Maguey Vida Single Village Mezcal

1 ounce Appleton Estate Signature Blend Jamaican Rum

½ ounce Pierre Ferrand Dry Curaçao

½ ounce Orgeat Works T'Orgeat Toasted Almond Syrup

¾ ounce freshly squeezed lime juice

1 orchid, for garnish

1 lime wheel, for garnish

1 mint sprig, for garnish

Combine all the ingredients, except the garnishes, in a cocktail shaker filled with ice and give a quick whip shake so as not to dilute the contents too much. Strain into a double rocks glass over crushed ice. Garnish with the orchid, lime wheel, and mint sprig.

PINK GHOST

BY CARLOS YTURRIA OF THE TREASURY IN SAN FRANCISCO, CALIFORNIA
SERVES 1

The Treasury, in San Francisco's Financial District, is set in a pretty formal space and the clientele tends to be serious. But, the staff don't take themselves too seriously—they sell heaps of Slushie drinks. Carlos designed the Pink Ghost for the Slushie machine, but you can also make it in a shaker.

A few years ago, he was down in Oaxaca with Steve Olson and a few other bartenders. They'd been drinking mezcal all day, then started on pulque. After that, things got crazy. They went to the edge of town to set off firecrackers Carlos had bought. I heard them shatter the night's silence in my room. I called Steve. "It's the middle of the night. What are you guys *doing*, man?!" Before they could answer, a police truck rolled by with a fifty-caliber machine gun on the back. The guys said they were headed back to their hotel, and the police left. Then, they set off one more. The truck started circling back toward them and they ran. I was pissed. Carlos knew it. He packed his things, certain he'd be sent home. The next morning, I lined them all up. "I get it, man," I said, pacing. "You guys are drunk, having fun. But you're firing fucking *rockets*, man!" They looked like such a sorry bunch, hanging their heads like dogs. The pulque made them do it.

1½ ounces Del Maguey Vida Single Village Mezcal

2 ounces strawberry puree or muddled fresh strawberries

1 ounce coconut milk

½ ounce freshly squeezed lemon juice

½ ounce honey syrup (recipe below)

1 spritz hemp oil

1 mint sprig, for garnish

Combine all the ingredients, except the oil and garnish, in a cocktail shaker filled with ice and shake until well chilled. Strain into a tall glass over crushed ice. Spray with hemp oil and garnish with the mint sprig.

NOTE: If making the recipe in a Slushie machine, add 1½ ounces water per serving.

HONEY SYRUP

Bring 3 parts honey and 1 part water to a boil in a pan, and then simmer until all the honey is dissolved. Let cool and store in the refrigerator for up to 1 month.

ENIGMA DE MUERTE

BY ANTHONY SCHMIDT OF FALSE IDOL IN SAN DIEGO, CALIFORNIA
SERVES 1

The experience of this cocktail starts with a pour of your favorite mezcal, Anthony's being Tobala, followed by a tropical sangrita-inspired drink. He's always loved how Mexicans eat—and drink. The bright, high-acid flavors—lime, salsa, agua fresca—to offset the richer flavors of mole or stewed meat.

Like others, Anthony got into mezcal because of Del Maguey. He says, "It opened my eyes to how different expressions can be made with the same species of plant and virtually the same method of production, but taste completely unique. To me, it was fascinating. I'm sure Ron felt the same fascination when he was out in the wilderness trying this stuff for the first time. The land it comes from has such an impact on the final product. You see the effects of place on wine, but rarely do you see terroir having such a huge impact in the world of spirits."

1½ ounces Siembra Valles Blanco

2 ounces freshly squeezed lime juice

1½ ounces passion fruit syrup

¼ ounce maraschino liqueur

¼ ounce Demerara syrup (recipe below)

1 ounce Del Maguey Tobala

Add all the ingredients, except the mezcal, to a blender with 1¾ cups of crushed ice. Blend at high speed for 2 or 3 seconds. (If you have no blender, shake vigorously in a cocktail shaker filled with ice.) Pour into a double old-fashioned glass and serve with a copita of Tobala on the side.

DEMERARA SYRUP

Combine 2 parts Demerara sugar with 1 part water in a pan over medium heat to dissolve the sugar. Do not boil. Once the sugar is fully dissolved, remove from the heat and let cool. Bottle and store in the refrigerator up to 1 month.

LIFE LESS ORDINARY

BY ALEX PROUDFOOT, FORMERLY OF CRAZY PEDRO'S IN MANCHESTER, ENGLAND

SERVES 1

Alex first served this drink in a handmade clay bowl with a sky-blue glaze inside. The clay, he said, represented the earth the maguey grows in, and the blue represented the sky and weather systems the plants thrive in. The drink was served with a bag of worry dolls to represent the people and cultures of Mexico. The bubbles on the surface of the drink when it's poured are a nod to how the palenqueros measure the alcohol content with the bamboo venencia: they read the perla.

1¾ ounces Del Maguey Vida Single Village Mezcal

¾ ounce melon syrup (recipe below)

½ ounce freshly squeezed lemon juice

¼ ounce crème de banane liqueur

½ ounce egg white

¼ teaspoon apple cider vinegar

1 wide swath of grapefruit peel, for garnish

Combine all the ingredients, except the garnish, in a cocktail shaker filled with ice and shake until well chilled. Strain into a second shaker without ice, and then pour into a chilled cocktail glass. For the garnish, hold the grapefruit peel aloft and express the oil by gently squeezing it, then rub the peel around the rim of the glass and discard.

MELON SYRUP

Combine 2 parts sugar and 1 part cubed honeydew melon and seal in an airtight container in a cool place. After a day or two, stirring intermittently, strain off the liquid and reserve, squeezing any excess juice from the melon pieces before discarding the pieces. Store in a sterilized bottle for up to 5 days in the refrigerator.

HIGH DESERT SWIZZLE

BY TOMMY KLUS OF LA MOULE IN PORTLAND, OREGON
SERVES 1

Tommy has never been able to roll his Rs, and this has always been a thing of comedy for me. He's tried for years, there are videos of him attempting it, he's even named cocktails with double-R names so he could practice at the bar. All to no avail. *Burro, perro . . . nada.* It's okay. He keeps trying.

Tommy came up with this drink during his time at Kask, in Portland. "Swizzle sticks had just come back into fashion and shrubs were finding their way onto menus," he says. "I wanted to use the snap of champagne vinegar with the sweetness of strawberry, while pushing forward the more earthy and vegetal tones of Vida." And it totally worked.

1½ ounces Del Maguey Vida Single Village Mezcal

¾ ounce freshly squeezed lime juice

¾ ounce strawberry shrub (recipe below)

¼ ounce Demerara syrup (page 244)

1 lime wheel, for garnish

Combine the mezcal, lime juice, strawberry shrub, and Demerara syrup in a highball glass. Fill it two-thirds of the way with crushed ice and swizzle like you mean it. The glass should frost up. Add more crushed ice, rounding out the top. Garnish with the lime wheel.

STRAWBERRY SHRUB

Wash and hull a pint of fresh strawberries. Weigh and place them in a flat container. Add an equal weight of evaporated cane sugar. Cover with plastic wrap and let the mixture sit overnight. The next day, when it's all gooey, add an equal part of champagne vinegar and mix to dissolve the sugar. Cover and refrigerate for another 12 hours. Once the sugar is incorporated, strain through a mesh strainer or cheesecloth. Bottle and store in the refrigerator for up to 6 months.

EL FUEGO DENTRO

BY MONICA BERG OF HIMKOK IN OSLO, NORWAY
SERVES 1

Monica was a tequila lover when she first tasted mezcal. She's always been into agriculture and traditional produce. In Norway, the national spirit is aquavit. It's made with caraway, which grows all over the country, so it's similar to mezcal in that it's tradition-bound. "I don't know if it's a coincidence, but there are only two spirits in the world that won't make me hungover: aquavit and mezcal," says Monica. "They're the two spirits I enjoy drinking the most, as well. Luckily, they go together beautifully!"

The name of this cocktail, she explains, reflects the passion of everyone involved with Del Maguey—as well as the warmth of the palenqueros. After traveling to Oaxaca, she told us she wanted to do something to support our producers and their families. She also wanted to see just how well mezcal and aquavit worked together. Faustino, in Chichicapa, had given her a few pieces of roasted piña, which she brought back with her to Oslo—technically, illegally. She distilled the maguey with a batch of aquavit that she makes in-house, using the maguey the way a chicken breast is used in pechuga. The results were blended with a little Chichicapa. She calls this hybrid Mezquavit. Every time they sell a shot of it, approximately one dollar is donated to a scholarship fund for the children of the palenqueros.

1½ ounces Del Maguey Vida Single Village Mezcal

½ ounce Linie Aquavit

½ ounce freshly squeezed lime juice

½ ounce red bell pepper syrup (recipe below)

Cilantro leaves, for garnish

Combine all the ingredients, except the garnish, in a cocktail shaker with ice and shake until well chilled. Double strain into a chilled coupe and garnish with the cilantro.

RED BELL PEPPER SYRUP

Combine 1 part cold-pressed red bell pepper juice and 1 part sugar and mix until the sugar is dissolved. Use immediately.

CHAMÁN

BY DAVID RIOS, COCKTAIL CONSULTANT AND EDUCATOR IN SPAIN
SERVES 1

Not long ago, nobody drank tequila in Spain—mostly because the quality of what was available was bad. Never mind mezcal, which was impossible to find. Nowadays, Spanish bartenders are loving Del Maguey, especially with Steve Olson traveling around the country offering workshops and classes to help them learn more about it.

When David first tasted our mezcal, he loved it immediately. He traveled to Oaxaca and describes it as one of the best experiences of his life. "I was in the middle of nowhere, in the mountains, with wild agaves. It was incredible," he recalls. "This cocktail is an ode to that place, that feeling. It's smoky, sweet, salty, and refreshing. I named it Chaman because drinking it will transport you to *México lindo*, like magic."

1¾ ounces Del Maguey Vida Single Village Mezcal or Tobala for extra complexity

½ ounce morita chile–infused Zacapa 23 rum (recipe below)

½ ounce shrimp mole syrup (recipe below)

1 ounce pineapple tepache (recipe follows)

1 pinch chapulín salt (page 237)

1 pineapple leaf, for garnish

1 morita chile, for garnish

1 pinch shrimp mole powder, for garnish

Combine all the ingredients, except the garnishes, in a copper julep cup filled with ice and mix using a miniature Mexican chocolate mill or *molinillo* (or substitute a swizzle stick). Garnish with the pineapple leaf, morita chile, and shrimp mole powder.

MORITA CHILE–INFUSED RUM

Add 6 to 10 morita chiles to a bottle of Zacapa 23 rum. Let sit for 24 hours, then strain and store indefinitely.

SHRIMP MOLE SYRUP

Combine 2 cups sugar with 2 cups water in a saucepan over medium heat until the sugar dissolves. Reduce the heat and add ¾ cup shrimp mole powder and a pinch of salt. Stir until combined, remove from the heat, and let cool. Store in the refrigerator for up to 10 days.

TEPACHE

Remove the skin from 1 pineapple, then clean and chop the skin. Combine the pineapple skin, 1⅓ cups brown sugar, and 8½ cups of water in a saucepan over medium-high heat until the sugar is dissolved. Transfer the contents of the saucepan to a large, clean glass jar or bowl and cover with a cheesecloth or towel. Let the mixture ferment for 4 to 7 days. Strain into a clean bottle and serve. Store in the refrigerator for up to 3 days.

ÁRBOL DEL TULE

BY NEYAH WHITE, MALT WHISKY BRAND AMBASSADOR AT PERNOD RICARD
SERVES 1

When I was a kid, going "out in the tules" mean going out to find some secluded place to fool around, the "tules" being weeds. But the word, like so many things in Southern California, comes from Mexico.

Neyah came up with this drink after he ran a Pineau des Charentes–focused cocktail list for six weeks at Nopa, in San Francisco. By the end of it, he had several bottles of the French aperitif left over and thought, *I'm never going to sell all this*. The answer was this refreshing highball, which turned out to be quite popular. He named it for the main attraction in a little town southeast of Oaxaca called Tule. It has a little church and the biggest tree you've ever seen. It's almost fifty feet wide—it takes a couple dozen people holding hands to encircle it. You stare at the tree, take a picture, buy something from one of the kids selling souvenirs, witness a miracle. There's nothing else going on. But it's a landmark in that part of Oaxaca.

1½ ounces Del Maguey Minero Single Village Mezcal

¾ ounce Pineau des Charentes

3 dashes orange bitters

1 ounce freshly squeezed orange juice

½ ounce freshly squeezed lime juice

Ginger beer, to top

Combine all the ingredients, except the ginger beer, in a cocktail shaker filled with ice and shake until well chilled. Strain into a highball glass over ice. Top with ginger beer.

JANE DOE

BY MIKE TOMAŠIC OF RHONDA'S IN SYDNEY, AUSTRALIA
SERVES 1

In 2011, there wasn't much information on mezcal available in Australia. But Mike managed to find us and arranged to come to Oaxaca for a visit. He arrived late at night, alone, on a small plane with fewer than a dozen people on it. No one spoke English and he spoke no Spanish. He didn't even have a phone number to call, just my address. He showed it to a taxi driver and they were off. The driver got lost and, pulling onto a dirt road, started yelling out the window to someone. Hearing stories about Mexico being dangerous, Mike thought he was about to get jacked. Finally, some time later, in the pitch black, they stopped in front of a house. My house. "Hey man, you're a long way from home!" I said to the most relieved-looking Aussie you ever met.

When I took him to Chichicapa, he and Faustino hit it off. Just before we left, Faustino came up to him with an envelope. Mike asked me what the contents read. "He's inviting you to his son's wedding in a few weeks," I told him, "but he understands if you can't make it." Mike went back home to Australia, worked for three weeks, then jumped on a plane all the way back again. He wasn't going to miss a traditional Zapotec wedding for the world.

This drink represents the holy trinity of spirit, amaro, and fortified wine—designed for the brave Negroni lover.

1 ounce ancho chile–infused mezcal (recipe below)

1 ounce Amaro Nonino

1 ounce Lustau East India Solera

1 tablespoon agave nectar

2 dashes Bittermens Xocolatl Mole Bitters

1 wide swath of orange peel, for garnish

Combine all the ingredients, except the garnish, in a mixing glass filled with ice and stir. Strain into an old-fashioned glass over ice. Garnish with the orange peel.

ANCHO CHILE–INFUSED MEZCAL

Rip apart 5 ancho chiles. Combine the skins and seeds with 1 bottle of Del Maguey Minero Single Village Mezcal in a jar. Leave it for 24 hours, then strain. Store indefinitely.

DR. FEEL GOOD

BY LEO ROBITSCHEK OF THE NOMAD AND ELEVEN MADISON PARK
IN NEW YORK CITY, NEW YORK
SERVES 1

When we asked Leo to come up with a cocktail, we braced ourselves. "Make it relatively simple," we said, "for the home bartender." But relatively simple is not what you go to The NoMad or Eleven Madison Park for. You go there to be enchanted, romanced, wowed. This drink, if you can pull it off, does just that. (You'll need an iSi Gourmet Whip or something similar for this one.)

1 ounce Del Maguey Minero Single Village Mezcal

¾ ounce fino sherry

¾ ounce avocado syrup (recipe below)

½ ounce Suze Gentian Aperitif

½ ounce freshly squeezed lemon juice

¼ ounce génépy liqueur

¼ ounce spicy agave syrup (recipe below)

1 cucumber slice, for garnish

Aleppo chile, for rimming the glass

Salt, for rimming the glass

Combine all the ingredients, except the garnish and rimming ingredients, in a cocktail shaker, add ice, and shake. Strain into a double rocks glass that has been rimmed with Aleppo chile and salt. Garnish with the cucumber slice.

AVOCADO SYRUP

Dissolve 2 cups sugar in 1 cup water in a large bowl. Combine with 2 cups of cubed avocado and 2 cups freshly squeezed lime juice and, using a hand blender, beat until very smooth. Pass through a chinois fine-mesh strainer. The syrup retains its color for 2 days when refrigerated.

SPICY AGAVE SYRUP

Dice, core, and seed 4 jalapeño peppers. Charge in an iSi Whip with 3½ cups hot water according to the manufacturer's instructions and let stand for 5 minutes. Pass through a chinois fine-mesh strainer and combine with 7 cups agave nectar. Store in the refrigerator for up to 2 days.

EL ÚLTIMO GUERRERO AZTECA

BY CARLOS SOTO, FORMERLY OF MAISON ARTEMISIA IN MEXICO CITY, MEXICO

SERVES 1

For Carlos, it happened backward, his introduction to mezcal. He's Mexican and was living in Vancouver when mezcal started gaining popularity. It was a Canadian who taught him about his country's national spirit. Growing up in Mexico City, Carlos saw mezcal as something his father and grandfather drank. It wasn't trendy. His parents were from Oaxaca, so it was part of their culture. When he returned to Mexico, after four years, he saw that people of all ages were drinking it. It was suddenly cool.

"I wanted to create cocktails that would resonate with the *onda* [vibe] of Mexico," he says. "El Último Guerrero Azteca is a variation on the Last Word, bringing together smoke, chocolate, honey, herbs, and citrus—quintessential Mexican elements. The name refers to the Aztec civilization of Tenochtitlán, now Mexico City, my birthplace.

"The thing I love about mezcal is that you have to take your time to enjoy it. To me, that's everything. The spirit has a high alcohol content—it's intense. If you don't take your time, you can get drunk easily. It almost forces you to slow down and appreciate it. We live in such a rush nowadays. Mezcal gives you the opportunity to savor life."

¾ ounce Del Maguey Vida Single Village Mezcal

¾ ounce crème de cacao white liqueur

¾ ounce Yellow Chartreuse Liqueur

¾ ounce freshly squeezed lemon juice

1 brandied cherry, for garnish

Combine all the ingredients, except the garnish, in a cocktail shaker filled with ice. Shake until well chilled and fine-strain into a chilled coupe or Nick & Nora glass. Garnish with the brandied cherry and serve.

RESURRECTION

BY VASILIS KYRITSIS OF THE CLUMSIES IN ATHENS, GREECE
SERVES 1

"I wanted to combine mezcal with Greek spirit and philosophy," says Vasilis. He does this by pairing mezcal and mastiha, a traditional Greek liqueur that hails from the island of Chios. It's made with the sap of the mastic tree, an evergreen shrub that grows in the rocky soil on the south side of the island. Mastic sap has been harvested for millennia and was used for digestive ailments by Hippocrates himself. The liqueur is delicately honeyed, with notes of resin and anise. "Your parents would take it after dessert," says Vasilis. "But nowadays, people are mixing it with tonic or putting it in cocktails." To your health, then.

1¼ ounces Del Maguey Vida Single Village Mezcal

¾ ounce Skinos Mastiha

1 ounce salted pineapple juice (recipe below)

¼ ounce agave syrup

½ ounce fresh lemon juice

3 dashes celery bitters

2 makrut lime leaves, for garnish

Combine all the ingredients, expect the garnish, in a cocktail shaker filled with ice and shake until well chilled. Double-strain into an old-fashioned glass over cracked ice and garnish with the makrut lime leaves.

SALTED PINEAPPLE JUICE

Combine 1 quart of fresh pineapple juice with 5 grams of rock salt until salt is dissolved. Store in an airtight container in the refrigerator for up to 2 days.

MINERO MILK PUNCH

BY JOHN GERTSEN OF ABV IN SAN FRANCISCO, CALIFORNIA

MAKES 1½ LITERS

Benjamin Franklin loved milk punch. He famously enclosed a recipe for it in a letter to the governor of Massachusetts in 1768. More than a hundred years later, bottles of Franklin's milk punch were found and, amazingly, it was still good.

John adapted his recipe from Mary Rockett's Milk Punch, introduced to him by cocktail historian David Wondrich, and served it regularly at Drink Fort Point in Boston. One of the ideas behind Drink Fort Point is to encourage people to drink communally—the bar wraps around the entire space so there's plenty of room to belly up. When I went to visit John there, he gave me a bottle of his Minero Milk Punch. It was clear and golden in color, with a mellow, dulce de leche sweetness. Theoretically, he said, it could last forever.

1 750ml bottle Del Maguey Minero Single Village Mezcal

1 medium to large pineapple, peeled, cored and diced

1 3-inch cinnamon stick, cracked

½ Madagascar vanilla bean, sliced lengthwise and scraped

1 quart milk (preferably raw cow or goat)

4 ounces agave nectar

8 ounces freshly squeezed lime juice

Combine the mezcal, pineapple, cinnamon stick, and vanilla bean in a large airtight container. Let it infuse for two weeks. Strain and reserve the liquid.

Heat the milk to 180°F in a very large pot. Add the agave nectar and stir. Add the lime juice and reserved infusion, and stir. Cover the pot and allow it to cool for approximately 2 hours.

Slowly pour the mixture through a large fine-mesh strainer into a clean container, catching any curds that may have formed. The liquid—whey—will be cloudy. Carefully strain it a second time, using the same strainer, into a clean airtight container, one cup at a time. This process is tedious as the strainer fills with solids and the liquid drips through slowly. Bottle and store the clarified punch for several months in the refrigerator. Serve chilled in a port glass.

EL CARTEL

BY MATTIA CILIA OF MIXOLOGY'S LIVING ROOM ACADEMY IN SICILY, ITALY
SERVES 1

"Mexico is one of the best places in the world, like Sicily, where I live," says Mattia. "The climate is similar, the food is similar, even the people are similar. Not too tall and a bit fat. But real. The biggest problem we have in Sicily is the Mafia, and it's the same in Mexico with the narcos. This cocktail is my tribute to Mexico, which is beautiful like Sicily, but marred by crime."

Mattia wanted to make a drink with his favorite mezcal, Tepextate. He envisioned not just a drink but a whole ceremony to go with it: a tray emblazoned with the image of Mayahuel, the goddess of agave, carrying a little cast-iron burner with smoldering coffee beans. The smoke represents mezcal, the union of maguey and fire. Next to the burner is a teapot. (This cocktail is not mixed with ice, but chilled using an ice bath, because "mezcal con agua no es mezcal.") The drink comes with a little aperitivo—because it was conceived in Italy, after all—of *chapulines* (grasshoppers).

1¾ ounces Del Maguey Wild Tepextate Single Village Mezcal

1¼ ounces cold brew coffee

¼ ounce Mayahuel syrup (recipe below)

2 dashes homemade Tabasco bitters (recipe below)

A handful of coffee beans, charred in a cast-iron pan, for aromatics

Combine all the ingredients, except the coffee beans, in a mixing glass with no ice and stir. Chill the mixing glass in an ice bath until frosted. Pour the contents of the mixing glass into a teacup—or, better yet, serve the drink from a teapot into a couple of copitas to share—with the smoldering coffee beans on the side.

MAYAHUEL SYRUP

Combine 1¾ ounces agave nectar and 1½ teaspoons Lapsang Souchong tea in a plastic water bottle. Squeeze it before sealing with the cap to get all the air out. Place in a pot of water over medium-low heat to a temperature of 145°F to 160°F for 30 minutes. Store in the refrigerator for up to 1 month.

TABASCO BITTERS

Combine equal parts Peychaud's Bitters and Tabasco sauce. Store indefinitely.

DULCINEA

BY MEAGHAN DORMAN OF RAINES LAW ROOM, DEAR IRVING,
AND THE BENNETT IN NEW YORK CITY, NEW YORK

SERVES 1

"I love a rich nightcap-style cocktail, like a dessert you can drink," says Meaghan. "Crema is perfect for this: it's full of mezcal flavors with a little extra sweetness and a hint of salinity, which plays nicely off the chocolate notes in this drink. The deep, dark flavors put me in mind of my first trip to Oaxaca, which was right around Día de los Muertos, a special time of year."

Meaghan was traveling with three other women. Their first stop was San Luis del Río, where we make Vida. She remembers looking around the palenque, seeing how the spirit was made, and thinking to herself, "How does this even make it to us?" She started running through the logistics in her brain—the one phone for the whole town, how remote the village was—and couldn't quite grasp how it manages to get made, let alone exported to the US. In Santa Catarina Minas, she was struck again by how remote the place is, how primitive the process of making mezcal. Don Lencho had never had a group of four women visit him before. He asked them to bless the roast for him and ended up christening the batch Cuatro Damas (Four Ladies).

1½ ounces Zacapa 23 rum

1 ounce cream sherry

½ ounce Del Maguey Crema de Mezcal

2 dashes Bittermens Xocolatl Mole Bitters

1 brandied cherry, for garnish

Combine all the ingredients, except the garnish, in a mixing glass filled with ice and stir until well chilled. Strain into a chilled coupe and garnish with a brandied cherry.

BEET HAPPENING

BY ALEXIS SOLER OF OLD GLORY IN NASHVILLE, TENNESSEE

SERVES 1

Alexis was a club bartender for much of her career. She wasn't looking to get into craft cocktails, but ended up finding herself among bartenders who were. When she opened her own bar with her sister Britt, they put this drink on their first menu after the two of them worked on it together. Alexis is drawn to colorful ingredients and few foods are more vividly colorful than beets. The smoke of the mezcal and sweetness of the beet come together with the tartness of the yogurt for a bold, nuanced, vegetal drink. Pretty, too. Savory, but citrusy, with a texture that sits nicely on the palate.

1½ ounces Del Maguey Vida Single Village Mezcal

1 ounce fresh beet juice

1 bar spoon Greek yogurt

½ ounce freshly squeezed lime juice

½ ounce agave nectar

1 generous sprig of dill

Combine the mezcal, beet juice, yogurt, lime juice, and agave nectar in a cocktail shaker and dry shake (without ice). Pour into a collins glass over crushed ice and garnish with the dill.

ACKNOWLEDGMENTS

First, I need to acknowledge my agent, Jonah Straus, who pursued me for what seemed like several years. If it were not for Jonah, this book project never would have begun.

And . . . my incredible writing partner, Chantal Martineau. Without our shared adventures and collaboration, this story would certainly not have been realized.

Huge thanks to the team at Ten Speed Press for taking on this project: Hannah, Kara, Jane, and especially our great editor, Emily Timberlake, for making my adventure a real book.

To all my dear friends who have certainly helped form me, and as a result, this tale.

And finally to my three *hermanos*—Michael Gardner, Jimmy Yeager, and Steve Olson—who are instrumental in launching and maintaining this Del Maguey project with me.

Thanks also to: Sandra, Sadie, Sydney, Sachiko, Shirley, Suzanne, Jody, Hilda, Bob, Rusty, Ruthy, Dina, Doug, David, Doug, Jim, Phil, Sean, Derek, Carlos, Michael, Thierry, Ganzer, Bob, Emmerson, Siggy, Gloria, Al, Nathan, Lil, Rocky, Joshua, Luca, Gabe, Pancho, Sergio, Mito, Machonit, Cosme, Faustino, Maximino, Paciano, Marcos, Emma, Asuncion, Concepcion, Marilu, Vida, Florencio, Luis, Luis Jr., Florencio Jr., Alejandrina, Espiridion, Juan, Armando, Ester, Rosa, Rogelio, Leopoldino, Beto, Laurentino, Bigote, Fernando, Roberto, Anastacio, Rigoberto, Abel, Pedro, Don Roberto, Alberto, Leo, Saul, Zenon, Adolfo, Antonio, Ismael, Luis, Jose, Francisco, Javier, Pedro, Victor, Felix, Cesar, Misael, Ana, Ines, Erika, Don Abel, Bonifacio, Lalo, Aurelio, Gilberto, Jose, Alfredo, Gabriel, Gonzalo, Samuel, Rigel, Reina, Tomas, Dale, Jill, Tony, José, Angel, Ellen, Miguel, Arturo, Sydney, Kenny, Happy, Doug, Les, Rick, Evan, Penny, Gregg, Rick, Javier, Kate, Misty, Eva, Miguel, Miguel, Don, Jason, Janice, Tim, Demetrio, Gaspar, Roberta Eric, Bill, Tony, Jon, Joe, Lance, Sandy, Gary, Garrett, Bob, Marissa, Don Michael, John, Michael, Jan, Fred, Susana, George, Neyah, Roscoe, Bob, Ed, Matt, Harry, Miles, Leah, Tom, Gabe, Joshua, Jacques, Alexandra, George, Alice, Berenice, Richard, Brian, George, Noel, Jeff, Jorge, Cesar, Cedd, Andy, Ed, Peter, Dean, R.C., Joel, Kevin, James, Peter, Ismael, Kate, Kate, Joseph, Roberto, Katya, Guillermo, Alejandro, Hugo, Douglas, Bear, Ellen, Ray, Walter, Alvaro, Toby, Ruth, Gus, Alona, Mark, Bob, Jose, Oscar, Henry, Guy, Amy, Patricio Marilyn, Nicola, Gandalf, David, Angel, Andres, Antonio, Celerino, Graciela, Lalo, Willy, Gisele, Evan, Evan, Bobby, Robert, Annie, Harrison, Peter, Marcel, Jasper, Brice, Tony, Jaime, Marco, Tigre, Giles, Victor, Celerino,

Sergio, Thomas, Tomas, Arnulfo, Andy, Albert, Martin, Martin, Angela, Martin,
Bill, Janice, Cara, Jo Ann, Ayn, Elyse, Stan, Ellen, Nancy, Eugenia, Eugenia, Andy,
Mona, Robbie, Maggie, Bob, Suzanne, Don, Jonathan, Jonathan, Adam, Lionel,
Elad, Maddy, Ryan, Jeff, Ajax, Pamela, Laddie, Dick, Joan, David, Barry, Joan, Diego,
Diego, Joel, Mario, Zahra, Morgan, Linda, Zenon, Matt, Phil, Art, Jaz, Christy,
Lux, Oliver, Jan, Zara, Rachael, Rosie, Virginia, Ulrike, Judith, Riko, Wendy, Billy
Al, Lynda, Martin, Alexandra, Alexandra, Debbie, CJ, Mike, Darya, Gina, Kinlock,
Tony, Helen, Folker, Benjie, Carpio, Dennis, Lisa, Claire, Henry, Florent, Romain,
Jon Anders, Dan, Dan, Andrew, Paul, Denny, Les, Peter, Stephanie, Genivieve,
Brent, Helen, Tony, Pam, Alan, Michael, Dave, Jim, Sue, April, Julie, Susan, Caroline,
Subie, Bob, Bob, Richard, Jaime, Lee, Jan, George, Jan, Rachael, Kristin, Joe, Chris,
Natalie, Boyd, Rose, Brooke, Mark, Steve, Stillman, Simon, Gaz, Mark, Rhonda,
gregory, Meghan, Daniel, Claudia, Kate, Gary, Lou, Michael, David, Treys, Carlos,
Felipe, Adam, Carina, Joshua, Carl, Aidan, Duggan, Randy, Volker, Tad, Florencio,
Carol, Jon, Blanca, Berta, Frank, Alejandro, Eric, Moxie, Mark, Celerina, Ines,
Aaron, Pavel, Rodrigo, Marko, Charlotte, Miles, Dick, Federico, Christina, Mattia,
Cindy, Dianne, Sue, Jean, Daniel, Chuck, Chuck, Guy, Natalie, Al, Jim, Clark,
Robin, Laura, Claudia, Ricki, Ricky, Jefferey, Clytie, Tom, Howard, Nancy, Marco,
Greg, Kit, Alexandre, Steven, Sean, Pietro, Romy, Craig, Alberto, Matthew, Marc,
Derek, Rob, Zoe, Dagny, Tim, Erick, Corazon, Don Javier, Don Michael, Juan,
Asis, Marcos, Peter, Nicholas, Julian, Quinn, Tom, Gordon, Craig, Lucia, Norma,
Joel, Marilyn, Fred, Becky, Neil, Rhiannon, Zara Jean, Donald, Davindra, Dan,
Paul, Celia, Cecelia, Dana, Dan, Darby, Marie, Brian, Olivia, Yorgo, Jillian, Mary,
Debbie, Debra, Claudia, Elsa, Gail, Celia, Clytie, Jody, Ria, Sandy, Dusty, Monique,
Jan, Wyn, Tandy, Maye, Joan, Ulrike, Marcie, Jill, Marie, Freddi, Sophie, Enrique,
Charles, Delfin, Sam, Desiree, Dextra, Ted, Cherie, Dick, Donald, Simon, Dora,
Carl, Edie, Mag, Denise, Paul, Andrew, David, Oliver, Jens, Cat, Sam, Sandy, Eric,
Pat, Katherine, Monique, Wendy, Cam, Jody, Dylan, Jackson, Houston, Janell,
Josh, Shaun, Jesse, Danielle, Tobin, Sharon, Joe, Marie, Emiko, Harlan, Emily, Jon,
Dushan, Camper, Guillermo, Tomas, Estevan, Eugene, Eusebio, Juliana, Ned, ole,
Freddie, Chris, Nick, Raul, Rodolfo, Arik, Larry, Freddi, Hank, Flojo, Tom, Barbara,
Ian, Stefano, St. John, Jay, Rob, George O, Mary Jane, Rubén, Dina, Bridget, Liz,
Tilton, Terry, Jo Harvey, Gary Paul, Agustin, Jennifer, Hubert, Doron, Hal, Gretchen,
Evan, Ricky, Guiseppe, Bale, Bukka, Jill, Benjamin, Pueblo Grande, Oscar, Adrian,
Abigail, Celso, Hanna, Harald, Harold, Lyndon, Kari, Ikuma, Rio, Susan, Alix, Max
III, Joanna, David, Dennis, Henry, Alba, Ian, Bobby, Roberto, Ulisis, Sandra, Manuel,
Charlie, Matt, Katya, Minette, J.O., Jack, Jacapo, Manny, Mali, Jacqueline, Pedro,

Joan, Joel, Jun, Ree, Justin, Kirstin, Trevor, Jason, Savanna, Judah, Fernando, Nacho, Kumi, Amado, Rip, Gael, Thierry, Enrique, Margaritte, Barbara, Singam, Eileen, Phillip, Ilana, Shaw, Kent, Tanny, Lauren, Livio, Laurent, Leonard, Alice, Peggy, Jim, Marty, Ruth, Joe, Margie, Richard, Leonard, Claire, Matilda, Linda, Luchita, Lee, Matteo, Annand, Lynda, Pam, Jordan, Donnie, Marcela, Marcy, Seth, Marja, Marlo, Gaston, Max, Wence, Sandra, Mary Buck, Tommy, Dwight, Jason, Matthew, Anne, Alex, Meibao, Mel, Dante, Marco, Silvia, Ivy, Tsuyoshi, Pablo, Rotraut, Gail, Akemi san, Tadashi san, Joe, Alexandre, Simon, Roger, Howard, Nancy, Ian, Alix, Sebastian, Jay, Guy, Dean, RC, Chuck, Bill, Justin, Jeremy, Vasilis, Alexis, Carol Sue, Johnnie, Christine, Nick, Jeff. Jerry, Sid, Joanie, and Rosamond.

—Ron Cooper

When Ron Cooper asked me to write a book with him, I knew it would be a singularly illuminating experience. But he also surprised me—with his warmth, his willingness to open up to me, his faith in my work. My deepest thanks to him for entrusting me with his story. This book could not have come together without the families in Oaxaca who make Del Maguey possible. Getting to know them and learning about their way of life has changed me in profound and unexpected ways. Gabe and Arturo made me feel like I was part of the team and offered invaluable insights into Oaxaqueño culture. Misty, Steve, and all the bartenders who contributed recipes were so generous in sharing their experiences with me. The patience and expertise of Emily, Kara, and everyone at Ten Speed were a true blessing. My mom, always the first read anything I write, has been an armchair passenger on this journey from the start. Finally, a book like this requires weeks away from home doing research and many, many late nights at a writing desk. My husband, Richard, has been my champion and refuge for the better part of a decade. My daughter, Rita, my sun and moon. Together, they are my world.

—Chantal Martineau

INDEX

Published in the United States by Ten Speed Press,
an imprint of the Crown Publishing Group, a division
of Penguin Random House LLC, New York.
www.crownpublishing.com
www.tenspeed.com

Ten Speed Press and the Ten Speed Press colophon are
registered trademarks of Penguin Random House LLC.

The photographs on pages 13, 19, 27, 29, 37, 45, 46, 52, 57,
72, 78, 132, 155, 197, and 198 appear courtesy of the author.

Library of Congress Cataloging-in-Publication Data

Names: Cooper, Ron, (Chef), author. | Martineau, Chantal,
author. | Toolan, Michael, 1972- photograper.

Title: Finding mezcal : a journey into the liquid soul of
Mexico with 40 cocktails : you don't find mezcal, mezcal finds
you / Ron Cooper with Chantal Martineau ; photography by
Michael Toolan.

Description: California : Ten Speed Press, [2018] | Includes
bibliographical references and index. |

Identifiers: LCCN 2017049167 (print) | LCCN
2017058276 (ebook)

Subjects: LCSH: Cocktails—Mexico. | Mescal. |
LCGFT: Cookbooks.

Classification: LCC TX951 (ebook) | LCC TX951 .C714
2018 (print) | DDC 641.87/40972—dc23

Hardcover ISBN: 978-0-399-57900-4
eBook ISBN: 978-0-399-57901-1

Printed in China

Design by Kara Plikaitis

10 9 8 7 6 5 4 3 2 1

First Edition